THE CHAMPIONS RESUME

DR. GBENGA MATHEW OWOTOKI

TABLE OF CONTENTS

ACKNOWLEDGEMENT 4

PREFACE 5

CHAPTER 1: THE IDENTITY OF A CHAMPION 6

CHAPTER 2: DIVINE CHAMPIONS IN HIGH DEMAND! 14

CHAPTER 3: THE MAKING OF A CHAMPION 20

CHAPTER 4: THE PLACE OF TALENTS IN BECOMING A CHAMPION 29

CHAPTER 5: THE IMPACT OF THE GIFTS OF THE HOLY SPIRIT IN
BECOMING A CHAMPION 36

CHAPTER SIX: HOW THE HOLY SPIRIT HELPED JESUS TO EMERGE AS THE
GREATEST CHAMPION 38

CHAPTER 7: SUSTAINING YOUR CHAMPIONSHIP STATUS 50

CHAPTER 8: WHY MANY CHAMPIONS DO NOT LAST 57

CHAPTER 9: NOTABLE CHAMPIONS IN DIFFERENT FIELDS OF
ENDEAVORS 63

CHAPTER 10: PRACTICAL LESSONS FROM THE LIFE OF CHAMPIONS 73

CHAPTER 11: PITFALLS CHAMPIONS MUST AVOID 81

CHAPTER 12: RECEIVING THE ANOINTING TO BECOME A CHAMPION! 89

CONCLUSION 95

REFERENCES 96

OTHER BOOKS BY THE AUTHOR 97

CONTACT DETAILS FOR THE AUTHOR: 98

ACKNOWLEDGEMENT

I cannot but appreciate everyone that have played one role or the other as I continue in my journey of Purpose. I thank God for the womb that "housed" me. Mum has been a great inspiration. She nurtured me early in the path of righteousness. Thank you mum.

Thank God for everyone that have lifted my hands and supported me. The Hephzibah and Mountaintop family. God has used you as an anchor. I appreciate you all. Greater days are here. For those that have impacted on my life and ministry. You mean so much to me. The Lord bless you.

I want to say a big thank you to my jewel of inestimable value. You have been my rock and backbone. I wouldn't have gotten this far without your support and encouragement. Love you plenty and to my boys Leslie and Lemuel, you give me so much joy and daddy loves you without bars.

PREFACE

There's no such thing as emerging a champion without a fight! A champion is a champion because they fought and won. He competes and emerges first. According to the Merriam-Webster dictionary, a champion is a winner of first prize or first place in competition; it also means one who shows marked superiority. So, basically, a champion is a victor who became one by competing in a race and emerging a winner. He is one who, after all the battle is over is still standing.

People don't just become Champions overnight. Becoming Champions comes with a great price. The sacrifices, the tears, the sweat and countless hours of being in the grind. When others are sleeping, Champions are awake burning the midnight oil. They are persistent, they are consistent. They don't mind working 10000 hours if it will bring them to that 1 hour that will eventually make them Champions. They are focused with their face set like a flint. This is an inspirational book that will spur you up to be all that God wants you to be. It highlights what it takes to be a Champion with focus on the sacrifice, price and regiment of the life of a Champion. This book mirrors the account of champions in various life endeavors and what they did and still do to become and remain Champions in their chosen fields and how we can glean a lesson or two from their lives. This book also looks at the role of talents, gifts, the Holy Spirit etc in raising Champions.

This book will bless you immeasurably as you read through its pages. As you learn the lessons from this book, I pray the Holy Spirit inspires you to be the very best in what you do...

CHAPTER 1:

THE IDENTITY OF A CHAMPION

Who is a champion from a divine standpoint?

Let's get into the Word of God for answers.

The book of Hebrews contains a catalog of people who strove and became champions. We'll look at a few of them, look out for the common denominators among them and then draw out a biblically guided definition of who a divine champion is.

Enoch

"Because of faith Enoch was caught up and transferred to heaven, so that he did not have a glimpse of death; and he was not found, because God had translated him. For even before he was taken to heaven, he received testimony [still on record] that he had pleased and been satisfactory to God."(Hebrews 11:5)

Abraham

"[Urged on] by faith Abraham, when he was called, obeyed and went forth to a place which he was destined to receive as an inheritance; and he went, although he did not know or trouble his mind about where he was to go.

"[Prompted] by faith he dwelt as a temporary resident in the land which was designated in the promise [of God, though he was like a stranger] in a strange country, living in tents with Isaac and Jacob, fellow heirs with him of the same promise.

"For he was [waiting expectantly and confidently] looking forward to the city which has fixed and firm foundations, whose Architect and Builder is God. (Hebrews 11:8-10)

Esther

Although Esther was not listed in the list of champions in Hebrews probably because of time which the writer of Hebrews talked about, the Bible nonetheless, catalogs her exploits in a dedicated book, called *Esther*. She discovered her assignment after Mordecai her uncle made her see the sinister plan which Haman the Jews' enemy was plotting. Haman had planned to kill every single Jew as a result of Mordecai's refusal to reverence him. It would have been fine to deal with Mordecai, the Jewish culprit, alone but Haman wasn't satisfied with dealing with Mordecai alone, he wanted to deal with the entire Jewish community. Mordecai made Esther see this and challenged her to do something. The Bible provides the following account.

"Then Mordecai told them to return this answer to Esther, do not flatter yourself that you shall escape in the king's palace any more than all the other Jews.

"For if you keep silent at this time, relief and deliverance shall arise for the Jews from elsewhere, but you and your father's house will perish. And who knows but that you have come to the kingdom for such a time as this and for this very occasion?

"Then Esther told them to give this answer to Mordecai, "Go, gather together all the Jews that are present in Shushan, and fast for me; and neither eat nor drink for three days, night or day. I also and my maids will fast as you do. Then I will go to the king, though it is against the law; and if I perish, I perish.

"So Mordecai went away and did all that Esther had commanded him." (Esther 4:13-17)

Esther fearlessly carried out her divine assignment and emerged a champion.

David

"For David, after he had served God's will and purpose and counsel in his own generation, fell asleep [in death] and was buried among his forefathers..." (Acts 13:36)

King David was a revered king who fought many battles with the help of God and won them all.

Apostle Paul

"For I am already about to be sacrificed [my life is about to be poured out as a drink offering]; the time of my [spirit's] release [from the body] is at hand and I will soon go free.

"I have fought the good (worthy, honorable, and noble) fight, I have finished the race, I have kept (firmly held) the faith.

"[As to what remains] henceforth there is laid up for me the [victor's] crown of righteousness [for being right with God and doing right], which the Lord, the righteous Judge, will award to me and recompense me on that [great] day—and not to me only, but also to all those who have loved and yearned for and welcomed His appearing (His return)." (2 Timothy 4:6-8, emphases mine)

Apostle Paul gave his testimony about fighting a good fight, finishing his course and getting ready to receive the champion's crown, glory to God! Apostle Paul was a divine champion. Why? How? He fought the good fight of faith and finished his course.

Jesus Christ

"Therefore then, since we are surrounded by so great a cloud of witnesses [who have borne testimony to the Truth], let us strip off and throw aside every encumbrance (unnecessary weight) and that sin which so readily (deftly and cleverly) clings to and entangles us, and let us run with patient endurance and steady and active persistence the appointed course of the race that is set before us,

"Looking away [from all that will distract] to Jesus, who is the Leader and the Source of our faith [giving the first incentive for our belief] and is also its Finisher [bringing it to maturity and perfection]. He, for the joy [of obtaining the prize] that was set before Him, endured the cross, despising and ignoring the shame, and is now seated at the right hand of the throne of God." (Hebrews 12:1-2)

Jesus Christ, the greatest champion of all time ran the race set before him, endured the cross, despised the shame and emerged a champion.

So then, a champion is one who knows the Lord, discover their purpose and run their race successfully to the end.

The Common Denominators Among Divine Champions

Quality Walk with God

Every single champion listed in the Bible had a qualitative walk with God. The testimony about Enoch, for example, was because of his walk with God. He walked with God so much that God took him away, he didn't have to die. Abraham also walked with God. His walk with God made him leave his father's house in obedience to God's instruction to a place he didn't even know. Esther sent to Mordecai to tell the Jews to fast together with her for three days, after which she walked fearlessly into the king's palace which was not according to the law. That wouldn't have been possible with someone who doesn't have a qualitative walk with God. Apostle Paul's heart cry was *"that I may know Him"* (Philippians 3:10). That was a cry of someone who yearned for a qualitative walk with God. Jesus said, *"...I assure you, most solemnly I tell you, the Son is able to do nothing of Himself (of His own accord); but He is able to do only what He sees the Father doing, for whatever the Father does is what the Son does in the same way [in His turn].*

"The Father dearly loves the Son and discloses to (shows) Him everything that He Himself does. And He will disclose to Him (let Him see) greater things yet than these, so that you may marvel and be full of wonder and astonishment." (John 5:19-20)

Jesus also said,

"And He Who sent Me is ever with Me; My Father has not left Me alone, for I always do what pleases Him." (John 8:29)

"I and the Father are One." (John 10:30)

Faith and courage

Someone said that courage is not the absence of fear, but the ability to master fear. It takes a radical faith in God to do what Abraham did. In the natural, it will be considered the highest form of foolishness to leave a place with your family for an unknown place. Your wife asks you, "Honey, where are we going?" And then, you reply, "Sweetheart, honestly, I don't know, let's just keep going"! That was a big demonstration of absolute trust in God. It was this unshakable trust that made Abraham emerge a champion. Again, after many years of waiting on God for a child, Abraham finally got one in his old age and then God instructed again to sacrifice that one son! But Abraham's trust and faith in God was steadfast. He obeyed without questioning thus provoking God to pronounce mighty blessings upon him. Esther took her life in her hands and went in to the king which was not according to the law to plead the cause of her people. That was courage. David dared Goliath on the basis of his faith in and passion for God, and courage. Indeed, champions are courageous people.

A Sense of Purpose and Passion

There's no single person who emerged champion who wasn't consumed with a sense of purpose, mission and passion. The purpose and passion in their hearts were so strong that no barrier or opposition was strong enough to resist them.

Apostle Paul said:

"Both to Greeks and to barbarians (to the cultured and to the uncultured), both to the wise and the foolish, I have an obligation to discharge and a duty to perform and a debt to pay.

"So, for my part, I am willing and eagerly ready to preach the Gospel to you also who are in Rome." (Romans 1:14-15, emphasis mine)

Abraham saw the bigger picture. The Bible says "...he was [waiting expectantly and confidently] looking forward to the city which has fixed and firm foundations, whose Architect and Builder is God." (Read Hebrews 11:8-10). Once Esther caught the revelation of her assignment at the helm of affairs, she straightened up. Her uncle Mordecai had told her if she didn't do anything about the situation, deliverance would arise from another quarter, but she and her father's house would be destroyed. When she saw her purpose, she acted fast. Nehemiah was another shining example. He had a sense of purpose and mission. That purpose and passion in his heart made him sad to the point his boss the king noticed. The passion in his heart made him go all the way to rebuilding the broken walls of Jerusalem despite the stiff oppositions he encountered. He had tasks assigned for each day. What about Daniel? He purposed (or determined) in his heart that he would not defile himself, and as a result, he stood out (Daniel 1:8). Jesus kept his focus on the joy that was set before Him (Hebrews 12:2). Until you catch a revelation of the purpose of God for your life, you're not ready yet to become a champion! Ask God to show you what He would have you do. Say like Saul, "Lord, what do You desire me to do?" (Acts 9:6). Say also the inspirational prayer in Ephesians 1:17-18.

"[For I always pray to] the God of our Lord Jesus Christ, the Father of glory, that He may grant you a spirit of wisdom and revelation [of insight into mysteries and secrets] in the [deep and intimate] knowledge of Him, "By having the eyes of your heart flooded with light, so that you can know and understand the hope to which He has called you, and how rich is His glorious inheritance in the saints (His set-apart ones),"

The man of God Kenneth E. Hagin prayed those prayers more than a thousand times and grew in six months more than he had grown in fourteen years as a minister. He discovered precious things. Why? The eyes of his understanding got opened; he saw things he had never seen before. That encounter turned around his life and ministry.

Good Finishing

You are not a champion because you go to the warfront, no. You are a champion only if you return alive from the warfront. It is a serious catastrophe for an airplane to take off and not land successfully. So, as much as taking off is important, the landing is as also equally important. Apostle Paul declared his landing status thus: "*I have fought the good (worthy, honorable, and noble) fight, I have finished the race, I have kept (firmly held) the faith.*" (1 Timothy 4:7). Abraham, Isaac, Jacob, Joseph, and all the patriarchs up to Jesus Christ had a good landing.

So, here's the point: all champions have a good finishing.

CHAPTER 2:

DIVINE CHAMPIONS IN HIGH DEMAND!

A dire need for Kingdom champions today!

At no time in history has there been a very dire need for Kingdom champions than today. To keep you reminded, a kingdom champion is one who has a working relationship with Jesus Christ, has discovered their divine assignment and is walking in their divine assignment.

We are living in a very dangerous time when men and women are turning backs on God through abominable acts. We are living at a time in history when the church of Jesus Christ is not what it should be. These are times of severe lawlessness. Indeed, these are times we're experiencing the highest level of high-profile corruption of political leaders at the helm of affairs. The sworn enemy of the church has been on a vigorous assault more than ever before! These are days of unprecedented pandemic, the kind of pandemic the world has never experienced before. No doubt, these are the days when the sons of God are expected to manifest. This is the time when Kingdom champions are needed in the political sector, manufacturing sector, the world of sports, in the area of science and technology, finance and economic sector, agricultural sector, education sector, in the military, et cetera. The world is indeed experiencing a terrible mess and kingdom champions are needed to salvage the situation. The book of Romans reveals:

"For [even the whole] creation (all nature) waits expectantly and longs earnestly for God's sons to be made known [waits for the

revealing, the disclosing of their sonship].

"For the creation (nature) was subjected to frailty (to futility, condemned to frustration), not because of some intentional fault on its part, but by the will of Him Who so subjected it—[yet] with the hope

"That nature (creation) itself will be set free from its bondage to decay and corruption [and gain an entrance] into the glorious freedom of God's children." (Romans 8:19-21)

The prophet Obadiah also spoke about this.

"And deliverers shall go up on Mount Zion to rule and judge Mount Esau, and the kingdom and the kingship shall be the Lord's." (Obadiah 1:21)

Kingdom deliverers are the greatest need of the hour. God is looking for saviours who will rescue humanity from the grip of evil. My prayer is that God will find you worthy and reliable in Jesus' name.

Let me remind you about a particular tough time in the history of Israel as a nation. The Philistines had advanced, ready for battle against the Israelites. The Israelis also got ready. But then, a giant came from the camp of the Philistines to challenge the army of the Israelites. He challenged them to present one person to fight him. If he defeats the representative, the Israelites would become slaves to the Philistines, but if otherwise, the Philistines would become slaves to the Israelites. This wasn't supposed to be a serious problem, but then the physique of the giant was very intimidating. According to biblical account, the giant Goliath was a champion in his own right and his "height was six cubits and a span [almost ten feet]. And he had a bronze helmet on his head and wore a coat of mail, and the coat weighed 5,000 shekels of bronze. He had bronze shin armor on his legs and a bronze javelin across his shoulders. And the shaft of his spear was like a weaver's beam; his spear's head weighed 600 shekels of iron. And a shield bearer went before him." (1 Samuel 17:4-7).

Goliath was no mean man for he had fought many battles. The Amplified version of the Bible calls him a champion. Of course, he was a worldly champion. So, this worldly champion challenged the armies of God with impunity and he did this for forty good days! Can you imagine that? The Israeli army got greatly intimidated every single time Goliath came up. No one had the courage to step out to face Goliath.

Obviously, there was a vacancy for a kingdom champion who could not only match the worldly champion Goliath but also utterly defeat him. It was amidst all this that David came on the scene. His father had sent him to take some food to his brothers who were part of the army. When he got there, he ran into Goliath's deafening threat. That got him infuriated. "How could an uncircumcised person who has no divine backing whatsoever insult the armies of the living God?", he reasoned. No way! David couldn't take that! The lion in him arose. David's fearless stand soon became known to King Saul.

See the account:

"David said to Saul, let no man's heart fail because of this Philistine; your servant will go out and fight with him.

And Saul said to David, You are not able to go to fight against this Philistine. You are only an adolescent, and he has been a warrior from his youth.

"And David said to Saul, your servant kept his father's sheep. And when there came a lion or again a bear and took a lamb out of the flock,

"I went out after it and smote it and delivered the lamb out of its mouth; and when it arose against me, I caught it by its beard and smote it and killed it.

"Your servant killed both the lion and the bear; and this uncircumcised Philistine shall be like one of them, for he has defied the armies of the living God!

"David said, The Lord Who delivered me out of the paw of the lion and out of the paw of the bear, He will deliver me out of the hand of this Philistine. And Saul said to David, Go, and the Lord be with you!" (1 Samuel 17:32-37)

To cut a long story short, David eventually conquered Goliath. He cut Goliath's head with Goliath's own sword. Glory to God!

Places Where Kingdom Champions Are Needed

Kingdom champions are needed urgently in the following places.

Political sector

Are you a Christian? Is there the cry of destiny fulfillment in your heart? Do you have a heart for positive transformation of people? Do you sense being called into the political sector of your nation? Or, do you believe politics is not for Christians?

I want to let you know that kingdom champions are needed in our political sphere. The Bible says when the righteous rule, the people rejoice but when the wicked are in authority the people mourn.

It is not surprising to see many ungodly bills being passed into law today. The reason is simple: there is a dearth of divine champions. Will you sign up for the class of this special kind of champions? God's desire is that these champions take over the parliaments and decision-making platforms of nations to the glory of His name. Were there godly people in politics in the Bible? Absolutely! Joseph was made a Prime Minister in Egypt, and because of his appointment he was able to save generations from the peril of prolonged famine.

By the wisdom of God at work in his life, he offered suggestion for the preservation of food and actually did preserved those food crops for seven whole years! I doubt if they had the kind of food preservation technology we have today, yet he was able to preserve food for seven years. What about Daniel? At a time in Daniel's political career, he became one of the three presidents. Even out of these three presidents, Daniel was the most preferred. An excellent spirit was at work in him. (See Daniel 6:1-3). Daniel proffered solutions to national problems on a number of occasions. Let's talk about Nehemiah also. If you take your time to study Nehemiah, you will fall in love with this God-fearing politician. Nehemiah exemplified a life of service. If we have just half of Nehemiah-kind of people in politics, the world would be a better place. Nehemiah was a selfless, committed, discerning and prayerful leader.

See one of Nehemiah's writings:

"Also, in the twelve years after I was appointed to be their governor in Judah, from the twentieth to the thirty-second year of King Artaxerxes, neither I nor my kin ate the food allowed to [me] the governor.

"But the former governors lived at the expense of the people and took from them food and wine, besides forty shekels of silver [a large monthly official salary]; yes, even their servants assumed authority over the people. But I did not so because of my [reverent] fear of God." (Nehemiah 5:14-15, emphasis mine)

History has it that the founding fathers of the United States of America were strong Christians, and that was the basis of the foundation of the constitution the country had. The Bible was their guide. But quite a lot of tampering has occurred today. Why? The works of the ungodly, which is why kingdom champions are needed in politics.

The Business Place

I love one of the stories I read about John D. Rockefeller. He was a businessman who had a special place for God in his heart. He gave away several millions of dollars to charity and other worthy causes. Indeed, God's looking for people who will make waves in the business world for His glory. God's looking for people who will be a channel for the great blessings He will pour out; people who will be committed Kingdom financiers. (See Matthew 25:14-29

Education sector

This is one of the platforms where champions are needed to effect radical changes for good. The effort of the man of God Oral Roberts in the area of education is one that will never be forgotten. The healing evangelist built Oral Roberts University in obedience to God's instruction. Today, the University has churned out several intellectuals who are kingdom champions. The school doesn't just focus on intellectual training, it also focuses on the spiritual aspect.

Entertainment industry

The entertainment space is in a big mess at the moment. Children have learnt and are still learning several unethical things from watching TV, and as a result, they do unthinkable things. Music, movies and other entertainment operations are greatly polluted. Pornographic materials have become rife. There is therefore a serious need for Kingdom game changers. Are you ready!

All Spheres of Life!

Every single sector must be taken for Jesus. Sports, commerce, aviation, technology, must all be taken for the Lord Jesus! Wouldn't you rather enroll and see what it takes to become a kingdom champion?

CHAPTER 3:

THE MAKING OF A CHAMPION

Showcasing the processes

Someone once said that behind every star is a scar. What does that mean? One of the implications of this statement is that champions are made in the crucible of rigorous training.

The making of a divine champion is double-edged. There is the human side and there is also the divine input. Most times, some Christians make a gross mistake focusing only on the divine aspect and downplay the human part of the deal. On the other hand, some Christians focus on the human side and for some reasons refuse to leverage on the divine aspect. If you doubt the double-edged nature of the making process of divine champions, let's have some zooming in on King David.

Jesse David's Resume

David happened to be the youngest son of his family. Perhaps that was why he was the one entrusted with the responsibility of tending for the sheep.

God had previously sent the incumbent king on a national assignment of which he failed to carry out the assignment to letter. This got God annoyed and He decided to withdraw His presence from the king -- Saul. In fact, God began to look for a replacement for the incumbent king. So, God sends prophet Samuel to go anoint another king for Him from amongst Jesse's sons.

Prophet Samuel got there and was about to make a costly mistake by anointing Jesse's first born who had the physique of a king. But then God corrects him. God told the prophet, "*Look not on his appearance or at the height of his stature, for I have rejected him. For the Lord sees not as man sees; for man looks on the outward appearance, but the Lord looks on the heart.*" *(1 Samuel 16:7)*. As a result of God's correction of the prophet, Samuel made all of Jesse's sons, except David who was not around, to pass before him. None of them was the chosen. Perplexed, the prophet asked Jesse, "*Are all your sons here?*"

Jesse replied, "There is yet the youngest; he is tending the sheep." (1 Samuel 17:11). This brings us to the first crucial qualification on David's CV:

Hard work

David wasn't idle. No wonder the Bible declares, "*Do you see a man diligent and skillful in his business? He will stand before kings; he will not stand before obscure men.*" *(Proverbs 22:29)*. Diligence is one of the distinguishing features of champions. By hard work, I mean real hard work. Athletes spend hundreds of hours practicing for an event that will take place on a single day. As part of their training, they jog regularly, exercise, eat specific kinds of food, do all kinds of things that will help them emerge champions. If you carefully consider the people Jesus called, they were all occupied, doing something; they were not idle. Peter and Andrew were fishing when Jesus called them, James and John were also busy fishing when Jesus called them, Matthew was a tax collector, Luke a physician, Elisha was a plowman, Apostle Paul was a zealous lawyer, et cetera. Coming to contemporary examples, Enoch Adeboye was a Mathematician and lecturer who was vigorously working to become the youngest vice chancellor in Africa before he was instructed by God to go into full-time ministry, Kenneth E.

Hagin despite his having a disadvantaged childhood as a result of a serious organic heart condition still worked during the Great Depression immediately after he got healed by the power of God, Dr. T. L. Osborn was a workaholic, the list is endless. But it all boils down to the fact that diligence (on the human side) is a major factor in the making of champions.

Skillfulness

It seems to me that the major link connecting the spiritual world to the natural world is skill. The reason is: I don't care how much 'spiritual' you are, if you are not skillful, you can only be rich in the spirit realm but be very poor in the physical realm. In the making of champions and on the aspect of human responsibility, skillfulness is a major requirement.

Again, going back to see some details as a result of the searchlight we have decided to beam on David, you will discover that David was a skillful young man. He was very skillful at what he knew how to do. That brings a scripture to mind which says: "Whatever your hand finds to do, do it with all your might" (Ecclesiastes 9:10). So, David was very skillful in these areas:

Playing of instruments: As a result of God's departure from King Saul, an evil spirit troubled him and he needed a skillful player to play instruments so that he could get refreshed. While the king's servants were racking their brain on who to use, one of them remembered David. He declared, "I have seen a son of Jesse the Bethlehemite who plays skillfully..." (1 Samuel 16:18). You see, don't just be *a person* at whatever you do, but be *the person*. Don't just be *an* engineer, be *the* engineer. Are you a banker? Be *the banker*. Be uncommon. Do whatever you do with excellence. Be so highly skillful that you become irreplaceable. One of the components of David's curriculum vitae was that he played *skillfully*.

"Do you see a man diligent and skillful in his business? He will stand before kings; he will not stand before obscure men." (Proverbs 22:29, emphasis mine).

It does not cease to amaze me to see footballers earn so much in a single month. But why? The answer: skill. And acquisition of skills is directly related to hard work, isn't it?

Discipline

Someone said that discipline is the soul of an army which makes small numbers formidable. Apostle Paul said:

"Do you not know that in a race all the runners compete, but [only] one receives the prize? So run [your race] that you may lay hold [of the prize] and make it yours.

"Now every athlete who goes into training conducts himself temperately and restricts himself in all things. They do it to win a wreath that will soon wither, but we [do it to receive a crown of eternal blessedness] that cannot wither.

"Therefore, I do not run uncertainly (without definite aim). I do not box like one beating the air and striking without an adversary.

"But [like a boxer] I buffet my body [handle it roughly, discipline it by hardships] and subdue it, for fear that after proclaiming to others the Gospel and things pertaining to it, I myself should become unfit [not stand the test, be unapproved and rejected as a counterfeit]." (1 Corinthians 9:24-27, emphasis mine)

Discipline is a crucial factor in the making of champions. You will never find a true champion who is not disciplined. If you find one, it's just a matter of time, he'll lose his championship title. It takes a great deal of discipline to attain and sustain the championship status.

Samson was a champion, but he soon lost it because he could not discipline himself. So, it's not enough to be a champion, rather, remaining a champion is also as important, if not even more important than just attaining championship. The reason is that your title could be taken from you by someone who's constantly exercising self-discipline.

Quickly, let me inform you that there are areas where we need to exercise discipline. We must exercise discipline in the area of:

Our words:

Recently, I heard a news about a boxer who was penalized for making unsavory comments. While the lockdown in many countries of the world was still very tough, he released a video of himself training and punching a bag. Then, he was reported to have said that that was how men should deal with their wives if they did any thing wrong. That generated a lot of row and that made women begin to agitate for very stiff sanctions on the boxer. The boxer later apologized saying that he was just trying to make up something funny. He even pledged some amount of money to help fight domestic violence but all of that fell on deaf ears. What's the lesson? A great deal of discipline must be exercised in the way we talk. The Bible says death and life are in the power of the tongue (Proverbs 18:21).

Our attitude towards the opposite sex

Our attitude towards the opposite sex is just as important as our words. At a time in the life of David, he lost his championship title. The time was a period for kings to go to war. But for some reasons best known to David, he stayed back in Jerusalem. It's better to read the story just as it is. It's found in Second Samuel chapter 11.

"In the spring, when kings go forth to battle, David sent Joab with his servants and all Israel, and they ravaged the Ammonites [country] and besieged Rabbah. But David remained in Jerusalem.

"One evening David arose from his couch and was walking on the roof of the king's house, when from there he saw a woman bathing; and she was very lovely to behold.

"David sent and inquired about the woman. One said, Is not this Bathsheba, the daughter of Eliam and the wife of Uriah the Hittite?

"And David sent messengers and took her. And she came in to him, and he lay with her—for she was purified from her uncleanness. Then she returned to her house." (2 Samuel 11:1-4)

That was a touching emotional story about David's fall. David did not go to battle. This was an inaction. Then, while resting at home and deciding to stroll on his roof, he sees a woman bathing. He wanted her so badly that he threw caution to the winds. He intentionally lost all his sense of reasoning and discipline. That was an action that costed him a lot. It is oftentimes said that David never lost a single battle but that isn't totally correct, for David lost the battle over his own family by that very action. So, discipline is a very essential key in the making of champions.

Our attitude towards money

You are never a champion until you are disciplined in matters concerning money. Whether it is your own money or not, one of God's requirements for you is financial discipline. Many have made a shipwreck of their faith because of lack of financial accountability and discipline. It can be very saddening when you see champions become ex-champions because of lack of financial discipline. Ananias and Sapphiras had the potential of becoming a giant kingdom financier but they lost out because of lack of personal discipline.

Judas, one of Jesus' disciples lacked discipline in money matters and lost the opportunity of becoming one of the Twelve.

Our interpersonal relationships

God has created us be social and interdependent, and as such we must value every destiny relationship He brings our way. You never can tell who God has destined to lift you into your ordained height in life. David's relationship with King Saul's son, Jonathan, is worthy of note here.

"When David had finished speaking to Saul, the soul of Jonathan was knit with the soul of David, and Jonathan loved him as his own life.

"Then Jonathan made a covenant with David, because he loved him as his own life.

"And Jonathan stripped himself of the robe that was on him and gave it to David, and his armor, even his sword, his bow, and his girdle." (1 Samuel 18:1,3,4)

You will agree that apart from divine choice, David's relationship with Jonathan also paved the way for David to emerge king. The Bible tells us Jonathan stripped himself of the robe that was on him and gave it to David, and his armor, even his sword, his bow, and his girdle. That was a sign of transfer. Jonathan who was heir to the throne and was supposed to be the next king transferred, as it were, his kingship rights to David.

Now, let's look at the aspect of **divine input** in the life of David.

A Good Heart

"For the Lord sees not as man sees; for man looks on the outward appearance, but the Lord looks on the heart." (1 Samuel 16:7)

Someone's bent on taking your life and then suddenly you hear that the person is dead and then you tear your clothes and burst into tears. What kind of a heart is that? That's a good heart, the God-kind of heart. Someone came to David telling him he had killed Saul, thinking David would be happy and reward him, but the reverse was the case. David had him killed. Also, David had opportunities to kill Saul who had been chasing him around and was bent on killing him, but he did not. He would not stretch his hands against an anointed of God. That was a godly heart, and everyone should pray for this kind of heart. It is a heart God is looking for. No wonder God called David a man after his heart. Not only that, David would apologize for his sin whenever he was wrong; he had a contrite heart.

"My sacrifice [the sacrifice acceptable] to God is a broken spirit; a broken and a contrite heart [broken down with sorrow for sin and humbly and thoroughly penitent], such, O God, You will not despise." (Psalm 51:17)

Are you humble in heart? Are you humble enough to take corrections? Are you humble enough to apologize when you are in the wrong? Do you feel happy and pleased when something bad befalls your perceived enemies? Do you love God's people genuinely? Do you sincerely care about them? Are you interested in their prosperity? Do you have a heart that is dependent on God? Or, do you have other options and alternatives you are banking on?

The Anointing

Finally, after prophet Samuel got to know there was still a son of Jesse left who was not present with them at the moment, he sent for him. As soon as he arrived, God spoke to him to arise and anoint David.

"Then Samuel took the horn of oil and anointed David in the midst of his brothers; and the Spirit of the Lord came mightily upon David from that day forward. And Samuel arose and went to Ramah." (1 Samuel 16:13)

Apart from David's own personal preparation, there was also the divine preparation. God had him anointed, and as a result the Spirit of God came upon him from that day forward! The anointing was also a distinguishing factor in the life of Jesus Christ.

"How God anointed and consecrated Jesus of Nazareth with the [Holy] Spirit and with strength and ability and power; how He went about doing good and, in particular, curing all who were harassed and oppressed by [the power of] the devil, for God was with Him." (Acts 10:38). The anointing of the Holy Spirit makes the difference. It is one of the key factors in the divine aspect of making champions. When one of King Saul's servants described David to Saul, he said: "I have seen a son of Jesse the Bethlehemite who plays skillfully, a valiant man, a man of war, prudent in speech and eloquent, an attractive person; and the Lord is with him." (1 Samuel 16:18). It couldn't have been just plain skillful playing that drove the evil spirit troubling King Saul away, God's presence must have been involved! David carried the anointing of the Holy Spirit, a mark of God's presence.

"Once You spoke in a vision to Your devoted ones and said, I have endowed one who is mighty [a hero, giving him the power to help— to be a champion for Israel]; I have exalted one chosen from among the people." (Psalm 89:19, emphasis mine)

CHAPTER 4:

THE PLACE OF TALENTS IN BECOMING A CHAMPION

Talents are wonderful, none is insignificant!

Who would have thought that having a talent for football would mean much some twenty years ago? But alas, talented footballers today earn in a single month what many people wouldn't earn in three years! Who really cares about someone sleeping and having a dream? Any dummy can sleep and dream. Yet still, is interpretation of dreams supposed to be any big deal? But guess what! That's what turned a former prisoner overnight to a Prime Minister! You remember Joseph, right?

His seemingly insignificant talent of dreaming dreams started when he was a teenager. He had dreamt about his future and God's plan for his life.

"Now Joseph had a dream and he told it to his brothers, and they hated him still more.

"And he said to them, Listen now and hear, I pray you, this dream that I have dreamed:

"We [brothers] were binding sheaves in the field, and behold, my sheaf arose and stood upright, and behold, your sheaves stood round about my sheaf and bowed down!

"His brothers said to him, Shall you indeed reign over us? Or are you going to have us as your subjects and dominate us? And they hated him all the more for his dreams and for what he said.

"But Joseph dreamed yet another dream and told it to his brothers [also]. He said, See here, I have dreamed again, and behold, [this time not only] eleven stars [but also] the sun and the moon bowed down and did reverence to me!

"And he told it to his father [as well as] his brethren. But his father rebuked him and said to him, What is the meaning of this dream that you have dreamed? Shall I and your mother and your brothers actually come to bow down ourselves to the earth and do homage to you?" (Genesis 37:1-10)

Of course, Joseph got himself into trouble with his elder brothers. The jealousy was so strong that they conspired to kill him. Thankfully, somehow, they agreed not to kill him again but then sold him into slavery. While he was serving as a slave, he got into another trouble. This time, his master's wife wanted him [Joseph] to sleep with her. But Joseph wouldn't, for he feared God! How many today wouldn't see that as an offer! But not Joseph! In fact, his refusal to yield to Potiphar's wife's daily temptation and pressure led him to become a prison inmate. He had been lied against. But, glory to God, God's presence never left him alone. The king of the land [Egypt] where he was a slave also had two of his servants thrown into the same jail Joseph was. Those two servants -- the chief butler and the chief baker -- had offended Pharaoh. But while they were in the prison, they both had a dream in the same night.

Read the account in Genesis 40:5-21.

That talent became manifested even in prison. It was the chief butler who later remembered Joseph during a period of great difficulty. The king had just had a very strange dream and he required the service of an interpreter. No one, including the magicians, in his entire kingdom could decipher the strange dream. But that was to be the unveiling of Joseph's destiny, for the chief butler remembered him and mentioned him in the ears of Pharaoh.

Without fail, Joseph is brought forth and again he harnesses the talent in his life.

After interpreting Pharaoh's narrated dream, Pharaoh announced Joseph to be a champion!

"And Pharaoh said to his servants, Can we find this man's equal, a man in whom is the spirit of God?

"And Pharaoh said to Joseph, Forasmuch as [your] God has shown you all this, there is nobody as intelligent and discreet and understanding and wise as you are.

"You shall have charge over my house, and all my people shall be governed according to your word [with reverence, submission, and obedience]. Only in matters of the throne will I be greater than you are.

"Then Pharaoh said to Joseph, See, I have set you over all the land of Egypt.

"And Pharaoh took off his [signet] ring from his hand and put it on Joseph's hand, and arrayed him in [official] vestments of fine linen and put a gold chain about his neck;

He made him to ride in the second chariot which he had, and [officials] cried before him, Bow the knee! And he set him over all the land of Egypt.

"And Pharaoh said to Joseph, I am Pharaoh, and without you shall no man lift up his hand or foot in all the land of Egypt." (Genesis 41:38-44).

Read Genesis 37-50 for Joseph's full account.

Talking about talents, no single talent is without significance! Even if your talent is just only one, that single one is more than enough to land you into limelight! (See Matthew 25:14-30). That's one of the reasons why the Bible says whatever your hand finds to do, do it with all your might (Ecclesiastes 9:10).

Recently, I watched a video clip of a prominent man of God reputed to be one of the champions of the Kingdom. The video clip contained an annual programme that was being held by the church. In that service, the man of God brought up an elderly man to the podium. Guess what, he introduced this elderly man as his Principal when he was way back in the high school. This man of God specially thanked the elderly man for raising godly children among whom he was one. Speaking on that international platform in response to the introduction of the man of God, the elderly man said that was the highest honor he had ever had in his entire life.

Cultivate the Right Attitudes Towards Your Talents

Let me remind you again: no single talent is insignificant. Do you have a talent to counsel people such that they get solution to whatever might be troubling them? Look not down on it! You can emerge a special adviser to some top government official or become a consultant to nations!

The following are the attitudes you should have towards your God-given talents so you can emerge a champion.

Discover

What are those things you are naturally good at? For some, it's an ability to organize things and make them be in order. That's a leadership trait. Some have an eye for details, they can easily spot errors in writings. Some have a profound ability to write. No talent is small. Discover what you are gifted for. Discover those things you naturally flow with.

Develop

As soon as you discover your talents, you should start developing them. Your talents are like raw gold that need to be processed before it can emerge shinning and truly useful. Remember, champions are made in the furnace of strict development. Your talents have to be honed or they become useless and unprofitable. Joseph must have spent time developing his talents of leadership and dreaming to another level of not just dreaming but interpreting dreams. The Bible also says he was left to keep charge of every prison inmate. That is leadership. Remember he had had to keep charge of Potiphar's empire. This preparation phase landed him on the championship pedestal. So, pay attention to every single talent in your life and be sure to develop them.

Deploy

Every talent multiplies with use but diminishes when out of use. It's wonderful to discover and develop your talents. But it's more wonderful and extremely powerful when you deploy them. Don't be afraid to fail or be criticized when you're trying to put your talents to work. Mistakes are part of the equation! Your path is ordained to shine brighter and brighter until you become a champion! Even if it will take you to begin by volunteering to work with your talents, please do, because the more you work on your talents the more it develops.

How You Can Leverage on Your Talents to Emerge a Champion

Let the fear of God reign supreme in your life

Allyson Felix is an Olympic runner. She is also a gold medalist. However, one astonishing thing about her is that she never takes the glory for any of the successes she has recorded so far. She ascribes all glory to God and trusts in the ability of God.

In fact, she uses her platform as a professional runner to promote the Gospel of the Lord Jesus Christ. She even ascribed her talent of running to God! That was exactly what Joseph did. When Pharaoh asked him if he could interpret dreams, saying that he'd heard he could interpret dreams, Joseph was very wise enough to direct that showers of encomium to God. Joseph declared, "...It is not in me; God [not I] will give Pharaoh a [favorable] answer of peace." (Genesis 41:16). The same Joseph was the one who said, "I reverence and fear God." (Genesis 42:18).

Constant development

Two times American national baseball champion, Tim Tebow spoke about how he was always on the go. If you truly want your talents to work magic and land you in the championship position, you must constantly improve on yourself. You must work on your talents, body, diet, and everything that impacts on your personal growth.

On the choice of diet, Tim said: "I've been following a low-carb, high-fat diet since late 2011/early 2012, and one of my biggest challenges early on was getting enough healthy fats and finding quick and convenient options as I am always on the go."

Faithfulness

Faithfulness will always be rewarded. Even when it's obvious you're not being recognized for what you do at the moment, faithfulness will help you in the long run. In spite of the circumstances at the time, Joseph did not fail to use his talents to be a blessing to others. You will remember that it was one of those who benefitted from the deployment of his talents who mentioned him before the king. So, use your gifts and talents to bless people, and do it faithfully. You may never tell who will connect you to your high places.

The Holy Spirit is the Biggest Leverage!

"*And Pharaoh said to his servants, Can we find this man's equal, a man in whom is the spirit of God?*" (Genesis 41:38, emphasis mine)

Even Pharaoh recognized the place of the Holy Spirit in the life of Joseph. Allyson Felix who was quoted earlier told *Christianity Today* "My speed is a gift from God, and I run for his glory". Allyson Felix, according to report, may be the fastest woman alive.

CHAPTER 5:

THE IMPACT OF THE GIFTS OF THE HOLY SPIRIT IN BECOMING A CHAMPION

Listen to the testimonies of Joseph, Daniel and others

It is so amazing to experience the tremendous impact of the gifts of the Holy Spirit in producing champions in any area of life. This impact cuts across different aspects of life. The gifts of the Holy Spirit in the life of its carrier work amazingly whether in career, business or ministry.

The gift of the word of wisdom catapulted Joseph from the prison to the limelight. It takes the gift of the word of wisdom to predict what will happen in the future and then make accurate plan concerning it. What brought Daniel to the limelight was the gift of God operating in his life. The King Nebuchadnezzar had had a very strange and troubling dream, and to make matters worse, he forgot the dream. So, what's the dilemma? The king wants to know what his dream is, plus interpretation. You slept on your lovely bed after having a very nice dinner, and then you had a dream that bothered you. That wouldn't be any problem; all you needed to do was narrate the dream and then you get some interpretation. But this time around, you could not remember the dream. Instead, you wanted someone to 'remember' for you what *you* forgot! Weird, isn't it? And to add insult to injury, you threaten to kill the magicians, astrologers, and all the wise men if they couldn't remember *your* dream. That forced Daniel to seek God's face, and in a night vision God revealed the secret to him. This revelation was what brought Daniel to the limelight; his championship status emerged.

While Archbishop Benson Idahosa was a young believer, he heard his pastor preach that Jesus said we could cast out demons, heal the sick, cleanse the lepers and raise the dead. That amazed him. He asked from the pastor again to know if that was really true. His pastor affirmed it. Then Idahosa got on his bicycle and began to go from one house to another looking to see if he could get anyone that was dead. After some search, he finally came upon a place where a child had just died. He sought permission to pray for the child and he was granted the permission. To cut a long story short, he prayed for the child and the child came back to life. Then he left there looking for another dead person again.

He got another and also raised him back to life. That was the announcement Benson Idahosa got. The gift of special faith operating in his life made him a champion in his generation. What about Smith Wigglesworth? This man of God was a man of faith. He knew how to bring God on the scene whenever he needed something. According to account about Smith, he "was a straight-talking Yorkshire lad with little education, no training and no credentials, but he shook the earth with his miracle-producing faith. For four decades spectacular healings and deliverances followed his preaching of the Gospel in many nations of the world. Thousands were converted leaving new and revived churches everywhere he visited." My prayer for you as you read this book is that the Lord will enlist you in this kingdom of champions in the name of Jesus Christ. Generations yet unborn will continue to celebrate the grace of God in the lives of Oral Roberts, Kenneth E. Hagin, Kenneth Copeland, Gloria Copeland, T.L. Osborn, Kathryn Kuhlman, John Wesley, Enoch Adeboye, David Oyedepo, Reinhard Bonnke, Joyce Meyer, Allyson Felix, and a host of others.

CHAPTER SIX:

HOW THE HOLY SPIRIT HELPED JESUS TO EMERGE AS THE GREATEST CHAMPION

The Holy Spirit can help you too, and He will!

Who is The Holy Spirit?

The Holy Spirit is the Spirit of God. He is the third member of the God-Head (Trinity). He operates in a unified purpose with God the Father and the Son, Jesus. The scriptures testify of this in Matthew 3:16-17:

"And when Jesus was baptized, He went up at once out of the water; and behold, the heavens were opened, and he [John] saw the Spirit of God descending like a dove and alighting on Him.

"And behold, a voice from heaven said, This is My Son, My Beloved, in Whom I delight!"

This took place during the baptism of Jesus before He was commissioned into His ministry.

After He was immersed in the river Jordan, the Holy Spirit descended on Him like a dove and God the Father spoke out from heaven to testify about the Son. Right from the conception of Jesus to His birth, the Holy Spirit was involved at every stage of Jesus' life and ministry. The Angel who came to bear the news to Mary according to the Luke's account told her, *"The Holy Spirit will come upon you, and the power of the Most High will overshadow you [like a shining cloud]; and so the holy (pure, sinless) Thing (Offspring) which shall be born of you will be called the Son of God".*

The Holy Spirit, Who is the Spirit of God is seen in First Corinthians 2:11-12:

"What person perceives (knows and understands) what passes through a man's thoughts except the man's own spirit within him? Just so no one discerns (comes to know and comprehend) the thoughts of God except the Spirit of God.

"Now we have not received the spirit [that belongs to] the world, but the [Holy] Spirit Who is from God, [given to us] that we might realize and comprehend and appreciate the gifts [of divine favor and blessing so freely and lavishly] bestowed on us by God."

The Holy Spirit: God's Promise to You

Acts 1:4-5,8

> *"And while being in their company and eating with them, He commanded them not to leave Jerusalem but to wait for what the Father had promised, Of which [He said] you have heard Me speak. [John 14:16, 26; 15:26.]*

> *"For John baptized with water, but not many days from now you shall be baptized with (placed in, introduced into) the Holy Spirit.*

> *"But you shall receive power (ability, efficiency, and might) when the Holy Spirit has come upon you, and you shall be My witnesses in Jerusalem and all Judea and Samaria and to the ends (the very bounds) of the earth."*

Acts 2:32-33

> *"This Jesus God raised up, and of that all we [His disciples] are witnesses.*

> *"Being therefore lifted high by and to the right hand of God and having received from the Father the promised [blessing which is the] Holy Spirit, He has made this outpouring which you yourselves both see and hear."*

In scriptures above, Jesus spoke of the promise of the Holy spirit to us in Acts 1:5 and 8 and in Acts chapter 2, we see the fulfilment of that promise: "...*He has made this outpouring which you yourselves both see and hear*". **(Acts 2:33)**

Then in Acts 2:38 and 39, Peter told the people that the promise of the Holy Spirit was given to as many as believed.

"*And Peter answered them, Repent (change your views and purpose to accept the will of God in your inner selves instead of rejecting it) and be baptized, every one of you, in the name of Jesus Christ for the forgiveness of and release from your sins; and you shall receive the gift of the Holy Spirit.*"

"*For the promise [of the Holy Spirit] is to and for you and your children, and to and for all that are far away, [even] to and for as many as the Lord our God invites and bids to come to Himself.*"

The Holy Spirit Is a Person

The scripture describes the Holy Spirit in personal terms and not as an impersonal force or something abstract. He can be talked with. Jesus refers to the Holy Spirit as a Person in John 14:16: "...*And I will ask the Father, and He will give you another Comforter (Counselor, Helper, Intercessor, Advocate, Strengthener, and Standby), that He may remain with you forever"*

The Holy is a divine personality. Receiving Him is more than just an experience. He comes to live and to dwell in you and to make his home in you thereby, making Him someone you can relate and be intimate with as well. He has emotions, intellect and will. Scriptures says in Ephesians 4:30 that He can be grieved:

"And do not grieve the Holy Spirit of God [do not offend or vex or sadden Him], by Whom you were sealed (marked, branded as God's own, secured) for the day of redemption (of final deliverance through Christ from evil and the consequences of sin)."

He also speaks through various ways and means. He spoke to the church at Antioch about Paul and Barnabas.

"While they were worshiping the Lord and fasting, the HOLY SPIRIT SAID, Separate now for Me Barnabas and Saul for the work to which I have called them." (Acts 13:2, emphasis mine)

The Holy Spirit also spoke to Philip in Acts 8:29 (emphasis mine).

"Then the [HOLY] SPIRIT SAID to Philip, Go forward and join yourself to this chariot."

The Holy Spirit comforts, guides, teaches and intercedes for the saints according to the will of God. John 14:26 reveals: *"But the Comforter (Counselor, Helper, Intercessor, Advocate, Strengthener, Standby), the Holy Spirit, Whom the Father will send in My name [in*

My place, to represent Me and act on My behalf], He will teach you all things.

And He will cause you to recall (will remind you of, bring to your remembrance) everything I have told you."

Likewise in Romans 8:26 scriptures affirm that He is an intercessor.

"So too the [Holy] Spirit comes to our aid and bears us up in our weakness; for we do not know what prayer to offer nor how to offer it worthily as we ought, but the Spirit Himself goes to meet our supplication and pleads in our behalf with unspeakable yearnings and groanings too deep for utterance."

The Workings of the Holy Spirit

The day of Pentecost ushered in the fulfilment of the promise of the Holy Spirit. See Acts 2:1-4

And immediately the Holy Ghost came upon the apostles and all that were with them at the upper room, they became champions. They became empowered and emboldened to preach the message of Jesus fearlessly before multitude of people. Peter who was once timid stood up with the eleven other apostles and proclaimed the gospel of Jesus to multitudes of people. The message was so much filled with power that it singlehandedly won about three thousand souls to the body of Christ. That's the work that only the Holy Spirit can do!

"Now when they heard this they were stung (cut) to the heart, and they said to Peter and the rest of the apostles (special messengers), Brethren, what shall we do?

"therefore, those who accepted and welcomed his message were baptized, and there were added that day about 3,000 souls. (Acts 2:37, 41)

So, how did the Holy Spirit help Jesus become the Greatest Champion?

Having considered and understood the person and the workings of the Holy Spirit, it becomes pretty easy to see how the Holy Spirit was instrumental in helping Jesus become a champion in His earthly ministry. It is quite striking how intertwined the ministries of Jesus Christ and the Holy Spirit are and how much there is in the Bible about their intimate relationship.

There are three episodes in the relationship between Jesus' ministry and the Holy Spirit which gave Jesus all the edge and the encouragement needed to emerge as the greatest champion of all time. Each of the three episodes points a great transition.

From Jesus' conception in Mary's womb which was through the Holy Spirit (Luke 1:35). Then, He is anointed by the Spirit at the River Jordan when He was baptized by John and finally, He receives the Holy Spirit at His glorification and exaltation which He poured out upon His church. Let's go on to examine each one of these three episodes in the relationship between Jesus and the Holy Spirit...

At Conception

Jesus' championship journey began right from conception.

"Then the angel said to her, The Holy Spirit will come upon you, and the power of the Most High will overshadow you [like a shining cloud]; and so the holy (pure, sinless) Thing (Offspring) which shall be born of you will be called the Son of God." (Luke 1:35**)**

"Now the birth of Jesus Christ took place under these circumstances: When His mother Mary had been promised in

marriage to Joseph, before they came together, she was found to be pregnant [through the power] of the Holy Spirit.

"But as he was thinking this over, behold, an angel of the Lord appeared to him in a dream, saying, Joseph, descendant of David, do not be afraid to take Mary [as] your wife, for that which is conceived in her is of (from, out of) the Holy Spirit." (Matthew 1:18, 20)

The meaning of the above scriptures is that a human nature in form of a baby was wrought by miracle in the womb of the Virgin Mary; it was formed in perfect holiness without the input of any man. The incarnation of Jesus was totally the work of the Holy Spirit, He made Jesus transition from the Son of God to becoming the Son of Man. This supernatural conception of Jesus made it possible for Him to be the perfect sacrificial lamb that was needed to atonement and redemption of humanity from eternal peril and damnation. If Jesus were to be conceived by the intercourse between a man and a woman, He would not have been able to successfully become the Lamb of God that takes away the sins of the world and thereby emerging as the champion of the human race, there is every tendency that He would have failed right at the beginning of the whole plan of redemption of mankind.

The Holy Spirit is an intimate and ever-ready ally of anyone who's willing to engage His ministry. Even if your conception story wasn't spectacular as that of Jesus, you still have an awesome opportunity to fulfill divine destiny. Many people wait for the spectacular and in the process miss out the miraculous. In his autobiography *Just As I Am*, Billy Graham said he never felt a thing, emotionally speaking, when he gave his heart to the Lord Jesus Christ. But that didn't stop him from becoming one of the greatest evangelists and soul winners the world has ever had.

At Baptism

Yet another encounter took place when Jesus came of age. Before age thirty, He had performed no miracles, He had done no preaching. He lived a rather normal life with His earthly parents and siblings in Nazareth of Galilee (see Matthew 2:22-23). Then, He became ready to move into His public ministry and this led to the next great move of the Holy Spirit in His life. Scriptures record this event in Luke 3:21-22

"Now *when all the people were baptized, and when Jesus also had been baptized, and [while He was still] praying, the [visible] heaven was opened*

"*And the Holy Spirit descended upon Him in bodily form like a dove, and a voice came from heaven, saying, You are My Son, My Beloved! In You I am well pleased and find delight!*"

After this attestation by God the Father, it was spoken of Jesus as being led and empowered by the Holy Spirit. In Luke 4:1 the bible records Jesus as being "full of the Holy Spirit"

THEN JESUS, full of and controlled by the Holy Spirit, returned from the Jordan and was led in [by] the [Holy] Spirit.

Matthew 4:1 also records this event:

"*Then Jesus was led (guided) by the [Holy] Spirit into the wilderness (desert) to be tempted (tested and tried) by the devil.*"

The Holy Spirit led Him to the wilderness to be tempted of the devil and He was there fasting for forty days and forty nights. He was able to defeat the devil and his temptations by the help of the Holy Spirit. He emerged from the wilderness an undisputed champion, ready for the next stage.

Luke 4:14 tells us:

"Then Jesus went back full of and under the power of the [Holy] Spirit into Galilee, and the fame of Him spread through the whole region round about."

Furthermore, in Luke 4:18 Jesus himself says: *"THE SPIRIT OF THE LORD [is] upon Me, because He has anointed Me [the Anointed One, the Messiah] to preach the good news (the Gospel) to the poor; He has sent Me to announce release to the captives and recovery of sight to the blind, to send forth as delivered those who are oppressed [who are downtrodden, bruised, crushed, and broken down by calamity]"*

From this time on, Jesus' whole life is lived in the power of the Holy Spirit. As soon as Jesus became full of the Holy Spirit, He began to do miracles: healing, raising the dead back to life, casting out devils, preaching from town to town and villages to villages, etc.

Luke 4:33-41 records:

"Now in the synagogue there was a man who was possessed by the foul spirit of a demon; and he cried out with a loud (deep, terrible) cry,

"Ah, let us alone! What have You to do with us [What have we in common], Jesus of Nazareth? Have You come to destroy us? I know Who You are--the Holy One of God!

"But Jesus rebuked him, saying, Be silent (muzzled, gagged), and come out of him! And when the demon had thrown the man down in their midst, he came out of him without injuring him in any possible way.

"And they were all amazed and said to one another, What kind of talk is this? For with authority and power He commands the foul spirits and they come out!

"And a rumor about Him spread into every place in the surrounding country.

"Then He arose and left the synagogue and went into Simon's (Peter's) house. Now Simon's mother-in-law was suffering in the grip of a burning fever, and they pleaded with Him for her.

"And standing over her, He rebuked the fever, and it left her; and immediately she got up and began waiting on them.

"Now at the setting of the sun [indicating the end of the Sabbath], all those who had any [who were] sick with various diseases brought them to Him, and He laid His hands upon every one of them and cured them.

"And demons even came out of many people, screaming and crying out, You are the Son of God! But He rebuked them and would not permit them to speak, because they knew that He was the Christ (the Messiah)."

Jesus through the power of the Spirit performed signs and wonders (Acts 10:38, Matt. 12:28, Luke 4:18), He cast out demons by the Spirit's power and proclaimed the gospel. Just as He did not act on His own terms but by His Father's (John 5:19-20, 8:26-29), in the same way He was not driven by His own power and strength, but by the power of the Holy Spirit. Even though He was divine, His humanity needed the power of the Holy Spirit. He was a man who did not live by or rely on human power but by the power of the Spirit of God. And because of this, He succeeded where all the others had failed. He emerged a champion!

At Pentecost

"John answered them all by saying, I baptize you with water; but He Who is mightier than I is coming, the strap of Whose sandals I am not fit to unfasten. He will baptize you with the Holy Spirit and with fire" (Luke 3:16)

"For John baptized with water, but not many days from now you shall be baptized with (placed in, introduced into) the Holy Spirit." (Acts 1:5)

All through the gospels account of the ministry of John the Baptist, there was an expectation that Jesus would give the Holy Spirit to His followers and this became a reality few days after His ascension. Prior to His ascending, He told His disciples that they would receive the Holy Spirit few days after He had gone (Acts 1:5). And on the day of Pentecost, what had been long anticipated finally arrived (Acts 2:1-4); the Holy Spirit given to the church. The Holy Spirit, no doubt, helped Jesus tremendously in His championship journey. And since His outpouring on the day recorded in the Acts of the Apostles, the Holy Spirit has remained here with us, available to anyone whose heart is ready and open to receive His ministry.

The Holy Spirit Can Help You Too, And He Will!

Jesus could not have succeeded and emerged as a champion without the help of the Holy Spirit. The same way Jesus needed the Spirit, much more do we also need Him today to emerge as champions.

Jesus assured His followers in John 14:12, "I *tell you for certain that if you have faith in me, you will do the same things that I am doing.*

YOU WILL DO EVEN GREATER THINGS, now that I am going back to the Father."

He promised that YOU will do much more than He did while He was here on the earth and this can only be achieved by the help of the Holy Spirit. The Holy Spirit is available and ever ready to help you always and with Him, you will do exploits.

CHAPTER 7:

SUSTAINING YOUR CHAMPIONSHIP STATUS

It takes greater effort to remain at the top than it takes to get there!

Yes, it takes greater effort to remain a champion than it takes to become one! As a matter of fact, to go down or be nothing, all you need do is *nothing*! It is not enough to become a champion, you must know and do what it takes to *remain* a champion! I'm sure you must have heard of people who were millionaires or billionaires sometimes in the past but then later became totally bankrupt. That will not be your portion in Jesus' name! But, according to Sir Winston Churchill, responsibility is the price for greatness. There are things you must do.

Achieving a long-term success in any endeavor requires two things -- getting success and keeping it. To get success in any career or endeavor is not an easy task. Sustaining what you've got is even harder. It is one thing to get rich; it is another to stay rich. To accept to follow Jesus is one big success, to sustain remaining a Christian takes a lot of sacrifice. Achieving success in life seems a very arduous task that requires a lot of demand on one. However, sustaining success at any level is much more demanding than the process of achieving it.

As much as God is highly involved in your journey to becoming champions, He is also more keen and able to help you sustain the position of your championship rather than it dying out with the years. The Bible says in First Samuel 2:9:

He will guard the feet of His godly ones, but the wicked shall be silenced and perish in darkness; for by strength shall no man prevail.

The epistle of Jude also affirms that God is able to keep you from stumbling and sustain you to the very end-

1:24 *Now to Him [God] Who is able to keep you without stumbling or slipping or falling, and to present [you] unblemished (blameless and faultless) before the presence of His glory in triumphant joy and exultation [with unspeakable, ecstatic delight].*

The Holy Spirit has also been given to God's people to help them become champions and not only to become champions alone but to also remain as champions. John 14:16 tells us:

And I will ask the Father, and He will give you another Comforter (Counselor, Helper, Intercessor, Advocate, Strengthener, and Standby), that He may remain with you forever.

Now, as much as God has His part to play in sustaining you as a champion, which He has already done by giving to you the Holy Spirit as your helper, you also have you part to play in sustaining your championship status.

Apostle Paul provides us with an insight into what to do to retain our championship title. *"Do you not know that in a race all the runners compete, but [only] one receives the prize? So run [your race] that you may lay hold [of the prize] and make it yours.*

"Now every athlete who goes into training conducts himself temperately and restricts himself in all things. They do it to win a

wreath that will soon wither, but we [do it to receive a crown of eternal blessedness] that cannot wither.

"Therefore, I do not run uncertainly (without definite aim). I do not box like one beating the air and striking without an adversary.

"But [like a boxer] I buffet my body [handle it roughly, discipline it by hardships] and subdue it, for fear that after proclaiming to others the Gospel and things pertaining to it, I myself should become unfit [not stand the test, be unapproved and rejected as a counterfeit]. (1 Corinthians 9:24-27)

The passage above gives us some insights on ways to sustaining our championship status so it does not slip out of our hands or fizzle out with greater speed than it came. And, number one is **focus**.

To remain a champion, you must be focused, and one of the elements of focus is setting goals for yourself. Goal setting helps you have pursuits at every given point in time. Goal setting for every relevant area of your life keeps you relevant. And, when you have achieved your goals, you set higher goals.

I love Apostle Paul. He was a champion indeed! One of his guiding principles is:

"...but one thing I do [it is my one aspiration]: forgetting what lies behind and straining forward to what lies ahead,

"I press on toward the goal to win the [supreme and heavenly] prize to which God in Christ Jesus is calling us upward." (Philippians 3:13-14)

Recall also what he said in First Corinthians 9:26:

"Therefore, I do not run uncertainly (without definite aim). I do not box like one beating the air and striking without an adversary.

Number two insight is **discipline**.

It takes a great deal of discipline to retain success at any level. In fact, it takes discipline to press for the fulfillment of goals you set for yourself. The Apostle Paul in First Corinthians chapter 9 cited earlier explains that a competitor goes into strict training.

He beats his body, he is strained and stretched and yet he presses on. Such discipline is not a one-time affair, it takes constant practice and great deal of sacrifice. For the Christian who desires to sustain his status of a champion, discipline is absolutely necessary. Without discipline, you can never grow, develop or even mature in the things that has been placed in your hands to carry out.

The amazing stories of certain champions recorded in *God's Generals* by Robert Liardon are very touching. One would not but weep for some of them. The book *God's Generals* beamed a thorough searchlight on why some succeeded and why others failed. Some started the race, became champions but lost out as a result of indiscipline. There are several stories of sports people who were champions but later went totally down; they let down their guards and became undisciplined. Some became slaves of sexual immorality, drug abuse and other vices. I pray for you that the grace for godly discipline will rest upon you in Jesus' mighty name. Amen.

Another ingredient pivotal in the sustaining of your championship status is **character**.

Billy Graham said, "When wealth is lost, nothing is lost; when health is lost, something is lost, but when character is lost, everything is lost." How true! Gifts and talents aren't enough! If character is missing in the equation, then such a life is a disaster waiting to happen. I don't care to know how beautiful you are! You may even clinch the *Miss World* title, if you lack character it's only a matter of time before you go completely down! If you doubt this, ask the ex-Queen Vashti. She was a champion in her own right but soon lost her championship title to pride. There are people who are very proud; some lack financial or moral integrity; some lack good human relations. It's high time you identified any flaw in your character and start fixing it! Nothing good last in the hands of whoever lacks character.

King Saul in the Bible lacked the character to sustain the championship status God bestowed on him. In First Samuel 15:1-35, the Lord instructed Saul to go smite and destroy Amalek because of what they did to the children of Israel on their way from Egypt to the Promised land. King Saul went quite alright, but he did not carry out the instruction as the Lord had instructed. He did the assignment his own way.

Verse 8 tells us:

"Saul and the people spared Agag and the best of the sheep, oxen, fatlings, lambs, and all that was good, and would not utterly destroy them; but all that was undesirable or worthless they destroyed utterly."

Saul chose to disobey and dishonor God and as a result of this, God rejected him to continue to rule as king over His people. God also rejected his family. God transferred his championship title to David.

"THE LORD said to Samuel, How long will you mourn for Saul, seeing I have rejected him from reigning over Israel? Fill your horn with oil; I will send you to Jesse the Bethlehemite. For I have provided for Myself a king among his sons.

"Then Samuel took the horn of oil and anointed David in the midst of his brothers; and the Spirit of the Lord came mightily upon David from that day forward. And Samuel arose and went to Ramah." (1 Samuel 16:1, 13)

It takes one who has taken his/her time to develop a solid godly character to remain a reigning champion. And how does one build this character? The bible shows us how in the book of Second Peter

1:5-8.

"For this very reason, adding your diligence [to the divine promises], employ every effort in exercising your faith to develop virtue (excellence, resolution, Christian energy), and in [exercising] virtue [develop] knowledge (intelligence),

"And in [exercising] knowledge [develop] self-control, and in [exercising] self-control [develop] steadfastness (patience, endurance), and in [exercising] steadfastness [develop] godliness (piety),

"And in [exercising] godliness [develop] brotherly affection, and in [exercising] brotherly affection [develop] Christian love.

"For as these qualities are yours and increasingly abound in you, they will keep [you] from being idle or unfruitful unto the [full personal] knowledge of our Lord Jesus Christ (the Messiah, the Anointed One)."

Don't quit! Champions never quit and quitters never become champions. You must have an unflinching determination. The kind of steadfastness and perseverance that doesn't quit doesn't throw in the towel and never gives up. It pushes past fear, doubt and unbelief and allows the pains and discomfort of growth to build a strong faith and an invincible spiritual might in you.

Second Corinthians 4:16 says:

"Therefore, we do not become discouraged (utterly spiritless, exhausted, and wearied out through fear). Though our outer man is [progressively] decaying and wasting away, yet our inner self is being [progressively] renewed day after day."

Lastly, rely on God and acknowledge Him in all that you do in your daily life because it is so easy to become sluggish and lose energy and vigor when things seem to be going wrong or not going as it should. Proverbs 3:5-6 says: *"Lean on, trust in, and be confident in the Lord with all your heart and mind and do not rely on your own insight or understanding.*

"In all your ways know, recognize, and acknowledge Him, and He will direct and make straight and plain your paths."

This implies praying for guidance and His help in everything and putting Him first in your life.

You need to have God at the center of your life if you truly want to retain your status as a champion. Remember, the most important place in life is to be in God's kingdom, to be part of God's family- that certainly guarantees God's constant help and guidance.

CHAPTER 8:

WHY MANY CHAMPIONS DO NOT LAST

How you can finish strong

The year 1945 was an absolutely unbelievable year for rookie evangelists. In that year, twenty-seven-year-old Billy Graham came storming out of seemingly nowhere to fill auditoriums across America, speaking to as many as thirty thousand people a night. Graham was hired as the first full-time evangelist for Youth for Christ, and his reputation as a uniquely gifted preacher roared across America like a prairie fire. The rest, of course, is history. You've heard of Billy Graham. But what about Chuck Templeton or Bron Clifford? Have you ever heard of them? Billy Graham wasn't the only young preacher packing auditoriums in 1945. Chuck Templeton and Bron Clifford were accomplishing the same thing— and more. All three young men were in their mid-twenties. One seminary president, after hearing Chuck Templeton preach one evening to an audience of thousands, called him "the most gifted and talented young man in America today for preaching."

Templeton and Graham were friends. Both ministered for Youth for Christ. Both were extraordinary preachers. Yet in those early years, "most observers would probably have put their money on Templeton." As a matter of fact, in 1946, the National Association of Evangelicals published an article on men who were "best used of God" in that organization's five year existence. The article highlighted the ministry of Chuck Templeton. Billy Graham was never mentioned. Templeton, many felt, would be the next Babe Ruth of evangelism. Bron Clifford was yet another gifted, twenty-five-year-old fireball.

In 1945, many believed Clifford was the most gifted and powerful preacher the church had seen in centuries. In that same year, Clifford preached to an auditorium of thousands in Miami, Florida. People lined up ten and twelve deep outside the auditorium trying to get in.

Later that same year, when Clifford was preaching in the chapel at Baylor University, the president ordered class bells turned off so that the young man could minister without interruption to the student body. For two hours and fifteen minutes, he kept those students on the edge of their seats as he preached on the subject, "Christ and the Philosopher's Stone."

At the age of twenty-five young Clifford touched more lives, influenced more leaders, and set more attendance records than any other clergyman his age in American history. National leaders vied for his attention. He was tall, handsome, intelligent, and eloquent. Hollywood invited him to audition for the part of Marcellus in "The Robe." It seemed as if he had everything.

Graham, Templeton, and Clifford.

In 1945, all three came shooting out of the starting blocks like rockets. You've heard of Billy Graham. So how come you've never heard of Chuck Templeton or Bron Clifford? Especially when they came out of the chutes so strong in '45. Just five years later, Templeton left the ministry to pursue a career as a radio and television commentator and newspaper columnist. Templeton had decided he was no longer a believer in Christ in the orthodox sense of the term. By 1950, this future Babe Ruth wasn't even in the game and no longer believed in the validity of the claims of Jesus Christ.

What about Clifford? By 1954, Clifford had lost his family, his ministry, his health, and then ... his life. Alcohol and financial irresponsibility had done him in. He wound up leaving his wife and their two Down's syndrome children. At just thirty-five years of age, this once great preacher died from cirrhosis of the liver in a run-down motel on the edge of Amarillo.

His last job was selling used cars in the panhandle of Texas. He died, as John Haggai put it, "unwept, unhonored, and unsung." Some pastors in Amarillo took up a collection among themselves in order to purchase a casket so that his body could be shipped back East for decent burial in a cemetery for the poor.

In 1945, three young men with extraordinary gifts were preaching the gospel to multiplied thousands across this nation. Within ten years, only one of them was still on track for Christ. To truly be a champion, it's not just about starting well, rather it's also about ending well.

So, Why Do Many Champions Not Last?

Let's consider some of the reasons why many champions do not last from the story of some champions who became ex-champions. My prayer for you is that you will never become an ex-champion in Jesus' mighty name.

Lack of personal discipline

The championship process is like a ladder and to climb up a ladder requires effort. There are certain things we do to go up in any area of life, whether in business, finance, career, ministry, walk with God or even personal life. But when we stop doing those things that got us up to where we are, then we start going down gradually. Our personal consecration is a good example. How many of us can honestly say the level of our personal meditation on the Word of God has increased since we gave our lives to Jesus?

Hasn't it gone down? Is our prayer life still what it used to be? What about our fasting life? What about personal holiness and fellowship with God? To be quite honest, these are sacrifices that make us and keep us as champions. Very many attain some levels of comfort and greatness and then relax. They feel they shouldn't take things too hard. Gradually they slide.

They become irritant to corrections. When David was running from one cave to another for his dear life, he never thought about adultery. But when he became comfortable and unsuspecting, he let down his guards and cooled off a little bit. His spiritual standing wasn't even any consideration for him, neither did he consider the consequences of the action he wanted to carry out.

Let me ask you: are you faithful to God and to your spouse? Who are you accountable to?

Pride

Pride, the Bible says, goes before a fall. When a person suddenly begins to feel he has achieved a lot by his own effort, pride has slipped in. When you can no longer be corrected, watch it, it is an element of pride. If you find it very difficult to admit an error and actually apologize, you are proud. When you allow your achievements to enter your head, you are on your way to undoing yourself.

Wrong company

The story of Chuck Templeton is a big lesson. He must have gotten in the wrong company for a promising and upcoming fire evangelist like him to have renounced his faith. The Bible tells us that evil communication corrupts good manner. (1 Corinthians 14:33). Samson got in the wrong company and ended up destroying his own life. Samson was such a promising champion. But he squandered his divine opportunities by getting along with the wrong company.

How You Can Finish Strong

Stay true to your personal consecration.

Maintain those things you did to get up. Ask for grace to sustain and maintain sacrifices required of you. Refuse to let down your guards and be aware you're being watched. Yes, some people are watching your lifestyle and are learning from you, whether you are aware of it or not. Be aware also that the heavenly witnesses are also watching you from the grandstands. See what Hebrews chapter 12 has got to say.

"Therefore then, since we are surrounded by so great a cloud of witnesses [who have borne testimony to the Truth], let us strip off and throw aside every encumbrance (unnecessary weight) and that sin which so readily (deftly and cleverly) clings to and entangles us, and let us run with patient endurance and steady and active persistence the appointed course of the race that is set before us" (Hebrews 12:1)

Let me keep this very simple: Your walk with God is everything! Out of your relationship with God streams or flows every other thing about your life. If you can't do much, it's totally fine. All that is required of you is one thing: keep your relationship with God in place, and other things will take care of themselves. Do whatever He tells you in your place of fellowship with Him and you'll be totally fine.

Be accountable

Never get to a place in your life when you are no longer accountable to anyone, never! Jesus said: "...I assure you, most solemnly I tell you, the Son is able to do nothing of Himself (of His own accord); but He is able to do only what He sees the Father doing, for whatever the Father does is what the Son does in the same way [in His turn]." (John 5:19).

So, Jesus was accountable to His Father God.

Summarily, the divine champions' race is not a hundred-yard dash, it is a long race. It is a marathon and marathon races don't require speed. They require grit, endurance, determination and ending well. Finishing strong is not impossible. It is going to take you to make some tough choices, personal brokenness and sticking out with God till the end in order to have a strong finish.

CHAPTER 9:

NOTABLE CHAMPIONS IN DIFFERENT FIELDS OF ENDEAVORS

Meet Biblical and Contemporary Champions and Join the List!

Champions are found all through the pages of the scriptures and in our contemporary world. They appeared in form of kings, warriors, prophets, doctors, statesmen, presidents, business moguls, political activists, apostles and judges. They were champions, ordained by God and they established His purposes on the earth.

1. Benjamin Carson

Benjamin Carson, popularly called Ben Carson is one person who is an inspiration to many. His success story transcends the medical field where he performed his major feats. Dr Ben was able to perform complex neurosurgical operations successfully, and he constantly attributes his success story to his mother and his rich relationship with God. An ability to separate conjoined twins joined head to head is no mean thing.

In a detailed story about Ben Carson's feat, the Washington Post report that, "… Carson frequently deploys anecdotes from his compelling life story — a hardscrabble childhood in Detroit, his climb to the Ivy League, his journeys through spiritual faith and advanced medicine…"

Ben Carson was indeed a champion in the medical field, and quite fortunately, success stories and secrets can be applied in any area of life.

2. Abraham – Hebrews 11:8-10, Romans 4:16-23

Abraham is referred to as the "Father of Faith" and that is because he chose not to stagger at the promises of God regardless of what he encountered.

When Abraham was 75 years old, God called him out to of his father's house to go a place where He would show him. He promptly obeyed and took his family and left the Ur of Chaldeans to the land of Canaan where he sojourned. (See Genesis 12:1-9). God further made an assuring covenant with him that he would have many descendants and a permanent homeland when he was still in the present childless condition and living as a stranger in the land of Canaan. Despite the difficult situation that Abraham was in, the bible records that:

"And he [Abram] believed in (trusted in, relied on, remained steadfast to) the Lord, and He counted it to him as righteousness (right standing with God)" (Genesis 15:6).

Even when all hope seemed lost and natural laws and conditions were against him and his wife Sarah to ever hope that they would bear a child, he still believed and trusted in what God had said concerning him and his future. Roman 4:17-23 reveals that Abraham's faith was unshaken; he did not consider the impotence of his own body which was as good as dead because of age or the deadness of Sarah's womb. Against hope, he believed in hope and did not stagger at the promise of God through unbelief and was fully assured that what God had promised He was also able to perform. What a great man with a faith so strong! Little wonder he was named the Father of Faith!

God eventually fulfilled His promise and Abraham had Isaac when he was a hundred years old after about twenty-five solid years of waiting. The child of promise was eventually born. Few years later, the Lord demanded that the child, Isaac, whom he had waited for for so long to be sacrificed unto him.

Pretty difficult, right? Imagine having to kill your only child with no hope of ever getting another, that's a lot difficult isn't it? One beautiful thing that characterised Abraham's life and made him a champion in his own right is his prompt obedience to the Lord's instructions. He did not bat an eyelid, and did as the Lord instructed him. He took Isaac to the mountain of Moriah the next day and was ready to sacrifice him. As he was about to slay him with a knife, the Lord stopped him from doing so. He had passed the test of the Lord excellently and God swore by Himself to make him great forever. And the promise came to fulfilment, even till today. His name will never be erased from the shores of history both with God and with men because he was a man who simply believed in the Lord.

3. Gideon (Judges 6:1-7,25)

Gideon was the fifth judge in Israel in the book of Judges. He was born at a time when the nation of Israel was going through oppression and hardship from the hands of the Midianities and this has been going on for seven years. It got so bad that the Israelites who were supposed to be the strongest people on the face of the earth were reduced to living in dens in mountains, caves and strongholds because of fear. It was at such a difficult time as this that the Lord raised Gideon to champion the deliverance of Israel from the hands of their oppressors, the Midianites. God never considered the fact that Gideon came from a poor family and was not a hero; He addressed him as "a mighty man of valor". The first task the Lord gave to him was to overthrow the altar of Baal that was erected by the people of Israel and then build an altar to God. He swiftly acted to the instruction of the Lord not minding what the people are going to do to him when they discover what he had done. That paved way to the major task of waging war against their oppressors. Interestingly, God reduced the number of volunteers from thirty-two thousand men to three hundred men.

Undaunted, Gideon prepared his men, each equipped with a lamp and a horn. And with their lamps and horns, and with God's help Gideon's army defeated their enemies who had a total of one hundred and thirty-five thousand heavily armed soldiers. Gideon's trust in God made him to be a champion in Israel and he ruled them for forty years.

4. Martin Luther (1483-1546)

Martin Luther was a German theologian whose writings inspired the Protestant Reformation. He was born on 10th November 1483, studied at the University of Erfurt and decided to join the monastic order in 1505. In 1507, he was ordained and began teaching at the university if Wittenberg. In 1510, he paid a visit to Rome and he was shocked at the degree of corruption he found there. His anger took a new turn about the clergy selling 'indulgences' that is a promised remission from punishments for sin, for someone still living or one who had died and was believed to be in purgatory. By the 31st of October 1517, he published his famous '95 Theses', calling out the papal abuses and the sale of indulgences.

He found out from the study of the bible that salvation is by faith and not through the effort of any man. This truth discovery pitched him against many of the major teachings of the Catholic Church. Within 1519-1520, he wrote series of pamphlets which further developed his discoveries- 'On the Freedom of a Christian Man, 'On Christian Liberty', 'On Babylonian Captivity of the Church, and 'To the Christian Nobility'. Through the help of the printing press, is writings and '95 Theses' spread quickly like wild fire through Europe. Due to the sparks of revival that his writings brought to the hearts of people in Europe, he began to face a lot of persecution from the leaders of the Catholic Church. In January 1521, he was excommunicated by Pope Leo X and then summoned to the Diet of Worms, an assembly of the Holy Roman Empire.

He refused to back down on the truths he had come to believe and this led to his being declared as an outlaw and an heretic by Emperor Charles V. He remained resilient even in the face of losing supporters. He started a vigorous work of translating the bible into German, underlining his belief that people should be able to read the bible in their own language and this translation contributed immensely to the development and spread of the German language. In 1534, he published the complete translation of the Holy Bible in German language.

5. John D. Rockefeller Snr. (1839-1937)

John came from humble beginnings in upstate New York. His father, William Rockefeller travels round the country peddling medicines and other wares while his mother, Eliza was a devout Christian whose job was to care for the family and the farm. John's father would later abandon his family and transferred the responsibility to John. He gave John money and told him to build a house for Eliza and the family, and then departed. He later received a letter from his father saying that he had married another woman. He refused to be dependent on his father; this made him to quit high school, completed a course at the commercial college and landed a job as an assistant bookkeeper. Two years later, he was promoted to chief bookkeeper and a year later, opened his own commodity commission house with Clark and Gardiner as his partners. One day, a man approached him in his store with a product he developed called kerosene. John became a partner and this became the beginning of his oil business.

The business grew by leaps and bounds as the economy began to boom after the Civil War. When the industry became plagued with challenges like falling prices and over production, he dealt with it by buying out his competitors and his partners. As he increased in wealth, he founded Standard Oil group in Cleveland which within a short period began to buy out its competitors until it controlled nearly all the refineries in Cleveland.

The company grew and dominated the oil industry so much that by 1911, John D Rockefeller had become the richest man in the world.

Rockefeller was also a strict Baptist and he maintained a strict ruling in his household where every bill was checked and the children had to perform chores to get their money. Their lifestyle never reflected how wealthy their father was. John practiced religious principles in the business world taking him on top of the list of the worlds' successful businessmen in his days.

He believed that the reason why God gave people wealth is so that they can use the wealth for the betterment of humanity. He turned into charities and benevolence in which he devoted himself completely to philanthropy. John's benefactions during his lifetime totaled into over 500 million dollars.

6. Oral Roberts (1918-2009)

Oral Roberts is a US evangelist who built a business empire and founded a world class university through broadcasting the Gospel of Jesus. He was born in Pontotoc County, Oklahoma and was the fifth and youngest child of Rev, and Mrs. E.M. Roberts. He spent two years of college study at different Bible schools in Oklahoma after he left high school.

During his lifetime, he started ministry from preaching in tents to preaching on the radio. He made his way eventually to preaching on the television and attracted a vast number of viewers.

Oral Roberts resigned from his pastoral ministry in 1947 and founded Oral Roberts Evangelistic Association. He has conducted well over 300 healing and evangelistic crusades on six different continents and has featured as a guest speaker in several national and international conventions and meetings.

He received a command from God to establish a university based on God's authority and the Holy Spirit. He dared to believe and obey God for this, despite not having been in any educational endeavor. His obedience and audacity gave birth to the prestigious Oral Roberts University in Tulsa, Oklahoma in 1963. The University received its approval in 1963 and had its first students in 1965.

Again in 1980, Oral had a vision of Jesus who encouraged him to continue the construction of the City of Faith Medical and Research Centre, which was commissioned in 1981. The building had three skyscrapers, of which the tallest called 'Cityplex Tower' stands at 198 meters with 60 floors. At the time, the City of Faith was the largest health facility in the world; its aim is to combine the power of prayer and medicine in the healing process.

Oral was also a pioneer televangelist and his broadcast attracted a large number of viewers.

He began broadcasting his revival programmes on television in 1954 and his television ministry continued with the Abundant Life programme having 80% of the US viewership by 1957. He founded Golden Eagle Broadcasting in 1996.

7. Robert Gilmore "RG" LeTourneau

RG LeTourneau is quite an interesting personality and is perhaps the most inspiring Christian inventor, businessman and entrepreneur the world has ever known. He went on from being a sixth-grade dropout to becoming the leading earth-moving machine manufacturer of his day having plants on four continents, major contribution to road construction and heavy equipments that changed the world forever and more than 300 patents to his name. However, his major and most important achievement is his contribution to the advancement of the Gospel of Christ which placed him among the greatest of Christian Businessmen of all time.

He was famous for giving 90% of his income to the spread of the Gospel and living on the remaining 10%.

RG is a great example of what a Christian businessman should be. He began working in an iron foundry at the age of 14 and he later discovered his love for machinery, he ventured into auto mechanic at first, and later as the manufacturer of the largest earth moving equipment on planet earth. Although there were many technological advances in other area of commerce in the early 1900s but in the area of earth moving, there was no invention at the time. Roads were still being built by engaging large numbers of men with shovels.

He was among the first road construction contractors to invent machinery to moving earth.

As a Christian, he felt the urge to do more for God. He went to meet his pastor for advice because he thought that anyone who was totally committed to Christ had to become a pastor or a missionary to truly fulfil the great commission. After a fervent prayer with his pastor, he was shocked to hear his pastor say the words that served as an anchor and guide to him for the rest of his life, "God needs businessmen too". He pondered on this new revelation and made a decision that his business would be in partnership with God.

In 1935, he had astronomical profits coming out of the manufacturing business and at the suggestion of his wife Evelyn; they made a decision to do a 90/10 split of their income with the Lord, 90% to the Lord and 10% to both himself and his wife. He was fond of saying,"It's not how much of my money I give to God, but how much of God's money I keep for myself." He founded LeTourneau Foundation to manage the administration of donations and by 1959, after giving 10 million dollars to religious and educational works; the Foundation was still worth some 40 million dollars. In his later years, he purchased airplanes from the profits of his business so that he could reach more and more people around the world.

LeTourneau was a mighty man of God whose life is a continual inspiration to Christians in the Business world today.

8. Enoch Adeboye

Enoch Adejare Adeboye is a mathematician and a pastor, popularly known as Pastor Adeboye. From very humble beginnings, the rise of this champion is a testimonial to the fact that there's absolutely nobody out of the reach of the Almighty God whom He can turn into a divine champion.

Adeboye's parents were so poor that he had no shoes to wear for the first sixteen years of his life. Somehow, Adeboye's eyes got opened to the fact that he couldn't really become great without a proper education.

Determined that he would never be poor like his parents, he began to study hard. He had a lofty ambition of becoming the youngest vice chancellor in Africa. In fact, he worked hard and became a lecturer. But as God would have it, he got born again and called into the ministry. Ever since, his story has been that of "from glory to glory". His salvation further helped him make astounding discoveries when he was working on his thesis. According to him, he discovered one day as he studied his Bible that just as God divided the Red Sea into two, he could also divide the myriad of equations he was battling with in his PhD work. That was how he made a headway in the project, thus making him earn a PhD in Applied Mathematics.

In 1981, he was appointed the General Overseer of the church where he got saved, and from the low beginning of the church, the church now has a physical presence in more than 190 nations of the world. God has used Adeboye tremendously and is still using him to perform signs and wonders across several nations of the world. Under his leadership, the church established a world-class university, several high schools and other numerous ventures.

Adeboye is so much revered even by politicians, not only in his country but also beyond. He is indeed a champion.

But guess what, the list is quite long and continuous. It is continuous because your name also needs to be added to the list! Receive grace for enlistment into the class of divine champions in Jesus' mighty name!

CHAPTER 10:

PRACTICAL LESSONS FROM THE LIFE OF CHAMPIONS

The secret of great men are in their stories.

Yes, truly, the secrets of great men are in their stories, and it is not just enough to read about stories of great men without being able to draw out lessons from their stories.

There are a whole lot of lessons that you can learn from them while you are on your journey to becoming a champion. Here are some lessons to draw out from their stories.

Obedience to Divine Leading

A critical look at champions both in the scriptures and in contemporary times shows that they were people who knew how to access, listen to and follow the leading of the Holy Spirit.

Kenneth Copeland had received a divine leading as a student to go work with Oral Roberts as his pilot. On getting to Dr Roberts' office, he introduced himself and asked to see him. But since he didn't book an appointment, it wouldn't be easy. Just then, Oral Roberts called out, "let him in". God had also told Oral that a student was coming who was going to be his pilot. That opportunity to work for Oral Roberts went beyond just being a pilot; he actually learned ministry practically, especially the healing ministry. That's one of the wonders of divine leading.

Abraham heard from God, thus leading him to promptly leave his father's house.

The end result is glorious, Isaiah heard God, David leveraged on divine leading in fighting wars, Ezekiel was thoroughly led, Apostle Paul was led by the Spirit of God, Kenneth Hagin was also thoroughly led by the Spirit of God, Jesus Christ was led as well. So, one key lesson from these champions is that they take the leading of the Holy Spirit very seriously. They do not take major steps in their lives without being led by the Holy Spirit. What great blessings lie in wait for you when you take obedience to God's instruction as essential as the air you breathe.

Vision

Another powerful lesson worth learning is vision. The Merriam Webster dictionary defines vision as the act or power of seeing. It is the ability to see beyond your present status and circumstances. Men who have made the list of champions are men of great vision. They saw beyond situations that surrounded them at the moment because they knew and saw something far greater than the present was ahead and this vision of a glorious future kept them going until they got to their final destination- the top.

I love the Oral Roberts' story. When God spoke to Oral Roberts to go build a university in 1963, it seemed like a mere word. He told Oral to "Raise up your students to hear my voice, to go where My light is dim, where my voice is heard small, and my healing power is not known, even to the uttermost bounds of the earth." God said those words to him about the kind of students he should raise when he didn't have a land let alone a school or a university. But he caught the vision and ran with it and today Oral Roberts University remains one of the foremost Christian universities in the world.

The same lesson can also be learnt from Joseph. At the age of seventeen God had started showing him the visions of his future. He saw himself becoming great and others coming to bow down to him.

He did not have the faintest idea of how such a vision would ever come to pass and even his own brothers and parents found it difficult to believe what God had said concerning his future. But alas, going through the story of Joseph we see how everything the Lord spoke to him about his future came to fulfilment. Joseph did not lose sight of the vision of his future even when he had to go through rough times - his own brothers conspired against him and sold him into exile far away from home, his master's wife framed him up and he was sent to jail for the crime he never committed, the person that was supposed to bring about his release from the prison totally forgot about him for two years. Yet through it all, Joseph kept his vision, he knew God had told him that he would be great, and he held on to it being persuaded that He Who had spoken is also able to bring it to pass. And it did happen; he became the Prime Minister of the most powerful country in the world at that time.

The book of Habakkuk 2:2-3 says: *And the Lord answered me and said, Write the vision and engrave it so plainly upon tablets that everyone who passes may [be able to] read [it easily and quickly] as he hastens by.*

For the vision is yet for an appointed time and it hastens to the end [fulfilment]; it will not deceive or disappoint. Though it tarry, wait [earnestly] for it, because it will surely come; it will not be behindhand on its appointed day.

These are important instructions by which many a believer might profit. God has an appointed time for all His purposes and their fulfilment. He cannot be hastened, for His schedule was made before the foundation of the world. When the appointed time comes, all visions will be accomplished. It hastens toward the end.

Humility

There was the story of a couple who both agreed to donate some of their fortune to a university. So, they took off and left for a particular university. They got there and sought an appointment with the president of the university. After waiting for what seemed like 'forever', they couldn't even get to book an appointment. So, they decided to go to another university. When they got there, they encountered the same thing. So, they decided to give a final try to yet another university. When they got there, they met some people working on some pipes. The couple introduced themselves and asked to see the president. The team leader of those working on the pipes offered them a seat and told them to give him just a moment to go inform the president. He went inside, quickly cleaned up himself, changed to a suit and came out and introduced himself to the couple, "You're looking for the president? I am the president. I had to get down to work on the pipes since they needed an expert on it and they couldn't find one and I knew about it perfectly." Impressed by this man's humility, the couple looked at each other in the eye and said, "We're in the right place." Then, they went ahead to donate some millions of dollars.

Pride is the undoing of many people today who would have become champions but never did. Also, pride is responsible for the fall of many champions, thus turning them to ex-champions. If you doubt this, ask Samson. Do you know that failure to acknowledge and rely on God is some form of pride? The Bible says that God resists the proud but gives grace to the lowly. God is the number one enemy of anyone who is proud. And when God becomes the enemy of a man, you know the end result. It will be catastrophic, isn't it? Pride has brought many anointed people down. I once read about an anointed man of God who worked with Evangelist Reinhard Bonnke. He was highly anointed of God in the area of the supernatural. Whenever Reinhard Bonnke finished preaching and 'wetting the ground', he would come up to pray for people and all kinds of miracles would happen.

But pride got into his head. One day, he decided not to show up for an already planned crusade. Of course, Bonnke, the key organizer of the crusade was unsettled. He sought God for help and God showed up. God moved very mightily and several unprecedented miracles took place. This man lost out. According to report, he would have been the one Bonnke would hand over to, but he lost his place to pride.

Diligence

This is another major common trait in the life of champions of every generation. They are people who are thorough, conscientious, and industrious. They are responsible and reliable and they make every effort to follow through on everything they start. To serve God requires much diligence without which you cannot really get much out of Him. The bible says in Hebrews 11:6 God *is a rewarder of those that DILIGENTLY seek Him* (Paraphrased). God's rewards cannot be gotten without diligence. The same principle also applies to your daily activities, career, business, marriage, et cetera.

R.G LeTourneau is a very good example of diligence. Through diligence and persistency and with divine help he was able to work his way through to the top. The fact that he was a sixth-grade dropout had disqualified him from ever smelling success or good fortune. As far as the world system was concerned, he was a loser. He was actually labeled as one who had no 'brain for school' and therefore was not amount to something good in life. But, against all odds, he rose through diligence to become the leading earth-moving machine manufacturer of his day having plants on four continents. The one who had 'no brain for school' literally designed sophisticated machines and wrote over 300 patents to his name. He became a public speaker also in the process and began travelling to different nations of the world to speak to people. Now, if RG could do it, you too can! There's no limit to what you can accomplish in life under God as long as you are diligent.

Following Your Passion

Passion is the enthusiasm and excitement for something or about doing something. It is a devotion to a particular activity that you enjoy doing. Every single champion had a strong drive that fueled their success and passion. Without passion for what you do or called to do, it is guaranteed that it is likely you die out on the way or veer off the track and keep repeating the cycle. It is very important that you find out what you are passionate about and pursue it with all that you've got. Your passion for what you do will be your drive and motivation to success.

RG LeTourneau discovered his love and passion for machines and he pursued it. Right from when he was fourteen, he started working in an iron foundry and later ventured into auto mechanics and from then on he knew the only place where he could function and be relevant is with the machines and today, he is reckoned amongst the world's foremost inventors of machines.

Likewise, Martin Luther also had passion for the truth of the word of God to be known and to spread to those who did not have access to it. He lived in a time when only the catholic bishops and the pope had access to the scriptures and whatever they said was what the people would believe, thus making people believe in a lie for years. This continued until Martin laid his eyes on the truth He didn't just keep it to himself; he made it known to the entire world the truths written concerning their salvation and justification in the scriptures, showing that it was not based on human efforts but purely a work of grace. Even though the entire church and the Pope himself was against him, he refused to recant the truth he had discovered. His passion for the truth to be known caused a spark of revival in the church and Protestantism was born. Not only that, he also translated the entire bible from Latin to German language and this helped in the development of the language. This made people to be able to read the Bible themselves and know what it says for themselves.

Patience

Life is in stages and phases, and success does not just jump at you. There are processes that you must go through, hurdles to cross, and challenges to face because each of these processes eventually becomes stepping stones into your greatness. The Bible enjoins in Hebrews 6:12: *That ye be not slothful, but followers of them who through faith and patience inherit the promises.*

Patience is a prerequisite to becoming a champion. Everyone who became a champion in their different fields of endeavor were taken through the journey of patience. Beginning with the story of Abraham and how he gave birth to Isaac, he had to wait for twenty -five years for a child! That certainly isn't easy. God called Abraham at the age of 75 and as of the time of his calling, he had no child and so one could have immediately thought that his childlessness was the first issue that God was going to address in his life but that was not the case. Instead of attending to his issue, God began to tell him that his descendants are going to be numerous on the face of the earth and that as no one can count the stars in the sky or number the sands, so would anyone not be able to number his offspring. Sounds crazy right? And even when God made that covenant with Abraham, one would have thought as well that God would make his wife Sarah become pregnant the following month. But no, it didn't go like that because there's a process that God had to take Abraham through. Abraham waited for 25 more years before he finally had Isaac. Now the period between God's promise at age 75 and the promise being fulfilled by the birth of Isaac at 100 years is the period of patience. Abraham waited patiently for the promise of a son which eventually came. That it took long does not mean that it would not come, it just requires that you be patient, follow and enjoy the process so that your testimony will be sweet and also serve as source of strength and encouragement to other people's faith.

Another inspiring story is the story of David. David is a man that is popularly known to be "a man after God's heart" God practically used his standard to measure the heart posture of all the Kings of Israel to determine which was successful before Him and who was not. How did David get to this level with God that he became God's standard for measuring other kings after him? One of the reasons is not farfetched though there are quite a number of others. Part of the reason is that David waited patiently on the Lord to lift him up to the throne by Himself. Now, David was anointed to be the next king of Israel at the age of seventeen when the Lord rejected Saul as king over His people. And from the time when he was anointed till the day he was crowned as the king of Israel, he never tried to usurp the incumbent king. Remember that David was anointed as the next king many years before the death of King Saul. He humbled himself and was loyal to Saul till the day of his death; he never lay claim neither was he arrogant. He also did not go on announcing to the entire world that God had made him to be the next king. If it were to be a man who is impatient that was in David's shoe, he would have organized a coup to take Saul out or even pray that God would kill Saul quickly so that he can sit on the throne. No, David never did all those, rather, he waited and followed through all of the process that God had to take him through before he became the king and he did not fall short. David didn't ascend the throne until he was thirty years old this means that he was patient and waited on the Lord's promises for thirteen solid years. Little wonder God said there would never cease to be a son from his house to sit on the throne. Kingship stayed in his household forever!

*For YOU HAVE NEED OF STEADFAST PATIENCE AND ENDURANCE, so that you may perform and fully accomplish the will of God, and thus receive and carry away [and enjoy to the full] what is promised. (*Heb. 10:36).

CHAPTER 11:

PITFALLS CHAMPIONS MUST AVOID

Identifying and avoiding the subtle dangers

A pitfall is a hidden or not easily recognized danger or difficulty. It is also a camouflage used to hold men. One can fall into a trap without even realizing it and there are surely a whole lot of pitfalls that can easily beset a champion and it is expedient that you are able to identify those pitfalls so that you do not fall victim of them. Most times Christians focus mostly on big and catchy sins like immorality, pride, dishonesty, et cetera. Although these are equally able to take one down but the subtle ones which we don't pay attention to have the ability to make one slide without even knowing it until it has happened. The scriptures say in Songs of Solomon 2:15:

Take for us the foxes, the little foxes that spoil the vineyards [of our love], for our vineyards are in blossom.

Foxes are crafty and subtle creatures, malignant and mischievous, hungry and voracious, full of deceit and dissimulation, they prefer to remain inconspicuous in a cozy, neat and organized place. So the 'foxes' in the above scripture are used as a metaphor to mean subtle sins which comes in to destroy the tender vine and prevent it from blossoming.

I will use stories of some champions in the Bible to show to you some of the subtle dangers that champions must avoid in order not to crash.

1. King Solomon

Solomon was the third king of the nation of Israel; he took over the kingdom from his father David and ruled for forty years. He was a king who enjoyed so much of peace and tranquility in his days so much that all through his reign as king of Israel, he never fought a single war. God made all of the other kingdoms to be at peace with him. He was also saddled with the responsibility of building the most beautiful temple that the world at that time had ever seen. He built the magnificent temple all laden with gold for God in Jerusalem and dedicated the temple in a grand style. Solomon had asked God for wisdom and God blessed him with so much wisdom that his fame and wealth spread throughout the world (1 Kings 10:14-29). God was with him in everything that he did and caused him to prosper and increase in wealth. He practically lived in affluence. As great, powerful and wise as King Solomon was, one weakness that he refused to deal with which in turn dealt with him and made him fell out of grace with God was that he "loved many strange women." He got married to the daughters of the nations which the Lord had given clear instructions for them not to marry from. The Bible has it on record that Solomon had seven hundred wives and three hundred concubines and his wife turned his heart away from the Lord. From the story of Solomon, *one of the dangers that a champion must avoid like a plague is disobedience to the word of God.* Solomon disobeyed the word of God by marrying strange women who converted him into idolatry.

King Solomon's neglect of the word, which at first appeared to have no bad effect (for he grew rich, as though it had been but the fulfilment of God's promise), soon led to a departure more serious in its nature and in its consequences, to influence more powerful and more immediately opposed to the commands of God's word, and at last to flagrant disobedience of its most positive and essential requirements.

The slippery path of sin is always trodden with accelerated steps, because the first sin tends to weaken in the soul the authority and power of that which alone can prevent our committing still greater sins-that is, the word of God, as well as the consciousness of His presence, which imparts to the word all its practical power over us. God brings chastening and trouble upon Solomon during his life and takes from his family the rule over the greater part of the tribes, declaring that He will afflict the posterity of David, but not for ever.

When we live our lives in obedience to the word of God no matter the height we get to in life, we can never be a victim of falling out of our position.

2. King Uzziah

King Uzziah's story is a must-read for any champion or anyone aspiring to become a champion. His story is very touching. (Read second Chronicles 26:1-21).

He began to reign at the tender age of sixteen and he reigned for fifty-two years. He started really well at the beginning of his reign, he sought the face of the Lord in everything that he does and God made him to prosper in everything he does. During his reign, the nation enjoyed remarkable growth and prosperity. He fought wars against the enemies and he won. His fame spread across the known world then. Verse 15 of Second Chronicles chapter 26 reveals that, *"And his fame spread far, for he was marvelously helped till he was strong."* King Uzziah was also an inventor. He invented machines to shoot arrows and great stones, built towers in Jerusalem and in the desert and fortified the cities and invested so much in agricultural and pastoral pursuits. He also had strong and powerful military forces, the number of his army totaled into three hundred and seven thousand and five hundred headed by two thousand and six hundred chiefs and the army are ever ready to help the king win a war against the enemy.

Unfortunately, when King Uzziah had grown very great and considerable in wealth, interest, and power, instead of lifting up the name of God in gratitude to Him Who had done so much for him, his *heart was lifted up to his destruction* and he transgressed against the Lord. Thus, the prosperity of fools, by puffing them up with pride, destroys them.

Now that he had done so much business, and won so much honor, he began to think no business, no honor, too great or too good for him, no, not that of the priesthood. Men pretending to forbid knowledge, and exercising themselves in things too high for them, owing to the pride of their heart, and the fleshly mind they are *vainly puffed up with.*

He went into the temple of the Lord to burn incense upon the Altar of Incense. His transgression was far more than we realize because it seems a small matter. The implication of his attempt to burn incense upon the Altar of Incense is that he proclaims the fact that he no longer needs God to do anything for him. He felt he had gotten to the peak of his reign and so he no regard his need for a savior. The moment a man begins to think that it is by his strength that he was able to achieve all that he has, without acknowledging God from that moment on; such a man begins his race to his downfall. Uzziah became a leper and died a leper. He was buried as an outcast in the field and not in the sepulchers of the kings.

The scriptures warned us about pride in the book of Proverbs 16:18-*Pride goes before destruction and a haughty spirit before a fall.*

How well it is for God's children to be much on their faces and humble themselves before the Lord. To be little in one's own eyes and make nothing of self is true greatness and the place of safety, where Satan stands defeated. There are so many stories of great men in history that show that the point at which a person is most vulnerable for a fall is at the pinnacle of their success or career.

This is because as we have seen from the story of King Solomon and Uzziah, they felt self-sufficient and took pride in the good works that has led to their elevation to the zenith of their career or reign.

3. Tiger Woods

Another illustration is the story of an internationally acclaimed golf player, Tiger Woods. In 2009, he was close to the zenith of his career and game but in 2010, some stories of a number of affairs was exposed to the world. His delinquencies were printed on the front-page headlines and trending stories on the news and after this, he never regained his professional and personal life. According to Roland Martin's *"Tiger, You Owe Me Nothing,* during his confession about his immoral relationships, he said: "I knew my actions were wrong but I convinced myself that normal rules didn't apply. ...I felt that I had worked hard my entire life and deserved to enjoy all the temptations around me. I felt I was entitled."

Danger begins to loom the instant a champion begins to think and believe that it is by his/her own doing that he/she is able to climb the ladder of success or possess great abilities and talents.

How to Avoid Dangers or Pitfalls

The truth is that as much as there are numerous stories of men who didn't pay careful attention on their way to the top and on getting there, they crashed, there are also testimonies of those that made it to the top and remained there without falling and they finished strong. A very good example of this is Joseph, the son of Jacob in the book of Genesis 39-41. Going through the story of Joseph, one would discover that Joseph followed through with God from the beginning to the end of his life without recording any failures.

Even when he was faced with a temptation from his master's wife in Gen 39:7-13, he never forgot the child of whom he was- the child of God. Verse 8 and 9 reveals Joseph's response to the seductions from his master's wife; he *refused and said to his master's wife, See here, with me in the house my master has concern about nothing; he has put all that he has in my care. He is not greater in this house than I am; nor has he kept anything from me except you, for you are his wife. HOW THEN CAN I DO THIS GREAT EVIL AND SIN AGAINST GOD?*

Another great example of a champion who had a strong finish is Daniel. He was of the royal seed in Israel and was captured by Nebuchadnezzar and was carried away to exile in Babylon. He was amongst the Kings seed chosen to serve king Nebuchadnezzar; they were to be colonized into the culture and the ways of life of Babylon. But Daniel and his three friends never forgot who they were nor where they came from and whose they were, they did not compromise with the rest of the king's seed by eating the delicacies from the King's table. God was also committed to them and he made them leaders even in a foreign land and Daniel outlived three kings of Babylon.

The first way to avoid pitfall is never to forget whom you are- Your Identity. Despite the fact that Joseph was sold into a foreign land and Daniel was also exiled into Babylon, they never forgot their identity. They always carried the consciousness of who they were and whose they were about their daily duties. Never forget that you are a child of God even in the face of temptation, don't give in to the lies of the devil that you can't overcome. Joseph did, Daniel did and so did Jesus you too can. The bible says in the first epistle of John chapter 4:4- *Little children, you are of God [you belong to Him] and have [already] defeated and overcome them [the agents of the antichrist], because He Who lives in you is greater (mightier) than he who is in the world.*

See what the word of God says concerning you- you are of God, you belong to God and so secured against infectious fatal delusions. You are His elect, and therefore cannot be finally and totally seduced; you are a child of God by adopting grace, and cannot become the servants of men; you are born of God, and so are kept by the power of God unto salvation, as all that are begotten unto a lively hope are; you are enlightened by the Spirit of God, and has a discerning of truth from error, and therefore sin cannot not be imposed on you.

The second way to avoid danger is to remain connected to the source- God! Never, ever lose touch of God no matter the level you attain. Joseph in the house of Potiphar in Egypt never forgot his source thus influencing his response to his master's wife when she tried luring him into sin that ... *how then can I do this great evil and sin against GOD?* Staying connected with God keeps you in constant reminder that you are not number one, God occupies that position in all that you do and say. When Joseph was brought before Pharaoh to interpret his dream, Pharaoh said to Joseph, 'I have a dream and there is no one that can interpret it: and I have heard of you that you can understand a dream and interpret it.' Joseph replied Pharaoh that, "It is not in me, God shall give you an answer of peace". Joseph could have claimed great things, but instead, he put God first and gave Him the glory. Even after Joseph had become the Prime Minister and second in command in the whole of Egypt and he had all the power at his disposal to punish his brothers for selling him into slavery to Egypt, he did not do that because his staying connected with God made him realize that it was all part of God's workings to send him ahead of time to preserve lives.

The third and final way to avoid pitfalls as a champion is that you must make a clear separation of the work you are called to do and the juicy rewards associated with it. You must never allow the material possession and the great amassing of wealth sweep your focus away from what you have been called to do.

As much as those things come by the virtue of the position you hold, you must never see them as personal rewards but as tools to do more and to accomplish your task. Daniel after God had helped him to tell and interpret king Nebuchadnezzar's dreams the bible says that: *then the king made Daniel great and gave him many great gifts, and he made him to rule over the whole province of Babylon and to be chief governor over all the wise men of Babylon. And Daniel requested of the king and he appointed Shadrach, Meshach, and Abednego over the affairs of the province of Babylon. But Daniel remained in the gate of the king [at the king's court]. (Dan 2:48-47).*

Daniel did not sit back and relax thinking that the Lord has finally lifted me up and it's my time to enjoy the riches, wealth and honor of Babylon even though he had them because he was appointed Prime Minister, the most powerful position in the world of that day other than the king himself, but no! Rather, he took his position as at the king's gate like a mere servant.

CHAPTER 12:

RECEIVING THE ANOINTING TO BECOME A CHAMPION!

Anointing is key!

Anointing makes all the difference in the life of a man or woman. There are speakers and there are anointed speakers; there are businesspeople and there are anointed businesspeople; anybody can do anything, but the anointing of the Holy Spirit makes all the difference!

The anointing is for empowerment. Contrary to what some believe, the purpose of the anointing is for empowerment, and not for show. The anointing adds *extra* to your *ordinary*, thus making it extraordinary; it adds *super* to your *natural*, thus making it supernatural. Truth be told, even though David was truly skillful, no amount of skill could have possibly brought down a veteran giant like Goliath! Something must be behind it! Yes, David had been tending the animals in the bush but prior to his being anointed no exploit was traceable to him. But immediately after he was divinely empowered by the reason of the anointing, he fought and killed a lion and a bear. After that feat, he went on to defeat Goliath. The secret is: "*Then Samuel took the horn of oil and anointed David in the midst of his brothers; and the Spirit of the Lord came mightily upon David from that day forward...*" (1 Samuel 16:13)

This same secret was behind the unimaginable exploits performed by Samson.

"Then Samson and his father and mother went down to Timnah and came to the vineyards of Timnah. And behold, a young lion roared against him.

"And the Spirit of the Lord came mightily upon him, and he tore the lion as he would have torn a kid, and he had nothing in his hand" (Judges 14:5,6)

The secret here was the Spirit of the Lord, Who is also the Anointer, praise God!

"The Spirit of the Lord God is upon me, because the Lord has anointed..." (Isaiah 61:1)

So, the Person Who anoints men and women and turn them to champions is the Spirit of God.

Elijah was a champion per excellence. He single-handedly challenged 450 prophets of Baal in a contest and put them all to shame. Indeed, the secret behind Elijah's exploits was the hand of God that was upon his life.

"The hand of the Lord was on Elijah." (1 Kings 18:46). You will agree that inside the hand of God lies His anointing. That was why Jabez told God: "... *Oh, that You would bless me and enlarge my border, and that Your hand might be with me, and You would keep me from evil so it might not hurt me! And God granted his request.*" (1 Chronicles 4:10, emphasis mine)

I want to get you ready and charged enough to receive the anointing of the Holy Spirit right where you are! Yes, right where are! All the members of the household of Cornelius got baptised in the Holy Spirit as they heard the Word of God being preached. Today is your day also! You can receive now, and if you're ready, receive the anointing of the Holy Spirit now in the name of Jesus Christ!

You need to appreciate the unique place of the anointing in the making of champions. Jesus never did a single exploit until he was anointed by the Holy Ghost. For about thirty years of his life, he was best known as the carpenter's son, nothing else. But as soon as he got the anointing, His fame went everywhere.

"Then Jesus went back full of and under the power of the [Holy] Spirit into Galilee, and the fame of Him spread through the whole region round about." (Luke 4:14)

The account in the Acts of the Apostles puts it this way:

"How God anointed and consecrated Jesus of Nazareth with the [Holy] Spirit and with strength and ability and power; how He went about doing good and, in particular, curing all who were harassed and oppressed by [the power of] the devil, for God was with Him." (Acts 10:38)

7 Things the Anointing Will Do for You!

- **The anointing of the Holy Spirit puts a unique touch on whatever you do.**

  The reason is, God puts His hand on whatever an anointed person does. In other words, whatever they do receives divine stamp. You'll recall Joseph's master's empire flourished in Joseph's hand so much that his master noticed it.

  "But the Lord was with Joseph, and he [though a slave] was a successful and prosperous man; and he was in the house of his master the Egyptian.

  "And his master saw that the Lord was with him and that the Lord made all that he did to flourish and succeed in his hand." (Genesis 39:2-3)

- **The anointing of the Holy Spirit will empower you and turn you to another person.**

  The moment the anointing came on Saul's head, the Bible says he was turned into another man. David's encounter with the anointing was that the Spirit of the Lord came upon him from that day forward. He later went on to kill dangerous animals, then Goliath and then later several enemies of the nation of Israel.

- **The anointing of the Holy Spirit promotes**

  "But my horn (emblem of excessive strength and stately grace) You have exalted like that of a wild ox; I am anointed with fresh oil." (Psalm 92:10). After the first anointing David received in the thirteenth verse of the sixteenth chapter of First Samuel, he got promoted and got anointed again in the fourth verse of the second chapter of Second Samuel as king over Judah.

  "And the men of Judah came and there they anointed David king over the house of Judah. They told David, The men of Jabesh-gilead buried Saul." (2 Samuel 2:4, emphasis mine)

  After this, David gets promoted to becoming king over the entire nation of Israel! Another promotion!

  "So all the elders of Israel came to the king at Hebron, and King David made a covenant with them [there] before the Lord, and they anointed [him] king over Israel." (2 Samuel 5:3, emphasis mine)

  The anointing of the Holy Spirit will promote you. Seek God and He'll anoint you in Jesus' name.

- **The anointing breaks yokes!**

  Glory to God! The anointing is a yoke breaker. A yoke is anything that limits or restricts. A yoke hinders people from making tangible progress. The man by the pool of Bethesda is a very good example. He'd been at a single location for thirty-eight solid years, down with lingering disorder. But Jesus, the Anointed with His anointing came to his rescue and healed him, thus destroying the long-standing yoke in the life of the man.

- **The anointing of the Holy Spirit protects and defends**

  "I have found David My servant; with My holy oil have I anointed him,

  "With whom My hand shall be established and ever abide; My arm also shall strengthen him.

  "The enemy shall not exact from him or do him violence or outwit him, nor shall the wicked afflict and humble him.

  "I will beat down his foes before his face and smite those who hate him." (Psalm 89:20-23)

  I'm sure if you have an opportunity to meet David and ask him some of the things he values the most, he'll tell you one of them is **the anointing!** The anointing protects and is a defense.

- **Favor is a product of the anointing**

   The psalmist confessed that the land the Israelites got wasn't by their swords and spears, but was purely by the favor of God. (See Psalm 44:1-3). In God's favor is life, and that comes by the anointing.

- **The anointing guarantees divine provision**

   The psalmist takes some time to carefully put up a very inspiring write-up about the provision of God and how it is linked to the anointing. (See Psalm 23:1, 5). Elijah the anointed was divinely provided for even during a severe period of famine.

How to Receive the Anointing

- ❖ Be born again. Without committing your heart to the Lord, you are not qualified for the anointing of the Holy Spirit.
- ❖ Live a holy life. Holiness makes way for and sustain the anointing.
- ❖ Get baptized in the Holy Ghost and start fellowshipping with the Holy Spirit regularly.
- ❖ Be in the Word regularly.
- ❖ Cultivate a lifestyle of worship.
- ❖ Obey the Holy Spirit promptly.

CONCLUSION

The entire world is in dire need of solution providers; champions actually. And, quite frankly, God is waiting on you!

"For [even the whole] creation (all nature) waits expectantly and longs earnestly for God's sons to be made known [waits for the revealing, the disclosing of their sonship]." (Romans 8:19)

While many of God's children are waiting on God to emerge champions to their world, God on the other hand is waiting on them to take responsibility and emerge champions. So, are you willing to take responsibility in paying the required sacrifices for the emergence of champions? Are you willing to be humble? Are you prepared to be disciplined in your words, thoughts and actions? The Lord will give you grace. The world is waiting for you, go and make impact in Jesus' mighty name!

REFERENCES

Kenneth E. Hagin, Holy Spirit And His Gifts. 1991, Kenneth Hagin Ministries, Inc. USA.

www.gpcweb.org/theHoly-Spirt-and-Jesus-Christ. 2020 Gainsville Presbyterian Church: Gainsville, VA

Steve Farrar. Finishing Strong; Going the Distance for Your Family. 1995, Multnomah Publishers.

OTHER BOOKS BY THE AUTHOR

- Mountaintop Boulevard - The Pilgrim's Journey into Bliss

- Don't Quit- Your Best Days Lie Ahead

- A Walk Into Eternity - An Inevitable Expedition of the Human Race

- Kingdom Attitude for Contagious Christian Living (ebook)

- Godpreneur – Tapping the God Principles That Framed The Universe

- 100 Days of Heaven on Earth...Warfare Prayer Guide

- Holy Ghost Fireworks – The Generational Workings of the Holy Spirit

- Kingdom for Sale – And the King Died

CONTACT DETAILS FOR THE AUTHOR:

Email: **gmattoki@gmail.com**

Facebook ID: **www.facebook.com/gbenga.owotoki**

Twitter: **www.twitter.com/GbengaOwotoki**

Instagram: **https://www.instagram.com/gbengaowotoki**

Made in the USA
Columbia, SC
06 July 2022

62897298R00059